NORTH STAFFORDSHIRE RAILWAY

ANTHONY DAWSON

AMBERLEY

First published 2023

Amberley Publishing
The Hill, Stroud,
Gloucestershire, GL5 4EP

www.amberley-books.com

ISBN: 978 1 3981 1443 2 (print)
ISBN: 978 1 3981 1444 9 (ebook)

British Library Cataloguing in Publication Data.
A catalogue record for this book is available from the British Library.

Typeset in 10.5pt on 14pt Celeste.
Typesetting by SJmagic DESIGN SERVICES, India.
Printed in Great Britain.

Contents

Foreword

In this engaging book, Anthony Dawson brings us the fascinating story of the North Staffordshire Railway – 'The Knotty'. From a wealth of research, with copious detail and great skill he guides us step by step: from the pre-history of early wagonways transporting limestone in the Moorlands, through its establishment during the railway mania of the 1840s to its successful eight decades of operation.

The main line sanctioned in the 1840s from London through the Midlands to Manchester and the North – the London & North Western Railway – bypassed North Staffordshire to its West. A population of a half a million people and an area abundant in mineral wealth – coal, limestone and iron ore – was left without access to the main rail network. The Knotty created lines from Stoke-on-Trent to link with the LNWR at Crewe to the north-west and Norton Bridge and Colwich to the south – and lines from Macclesfield via both Stoke and Leek to link with the Midland Railway at Willington. It expanded with 2,000 navvies, the clay extracted from cuttings making the bricks to line tunnels such as at Harecastle and build the viaducts at Congleton and Bollington.

Anthony gives us insight into every detailed aspect of the development, organisation and operation of this fondly remembered railway – serving its communities and travel further afield. He is rather like an expert horologist describing the intricate workings of some huge and magnificent timepiece. But then: the Knotty did run like clockwork, until it wound down a century ago.

Ray Johnson MBE, Staffordshire University

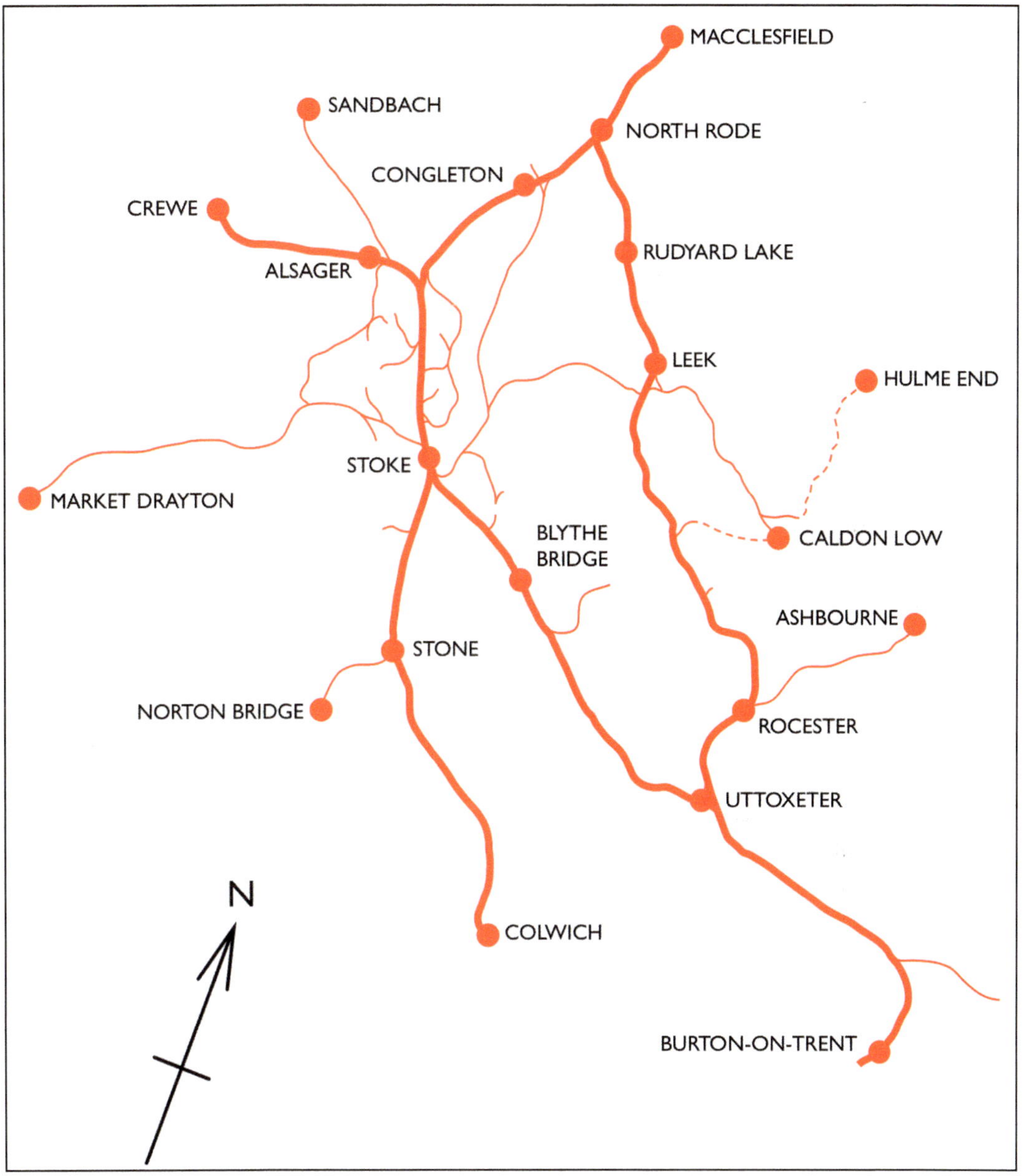

The North Staffordshire Railway was centred on Stoke-on-Trent, where the head office, locomotive and carriage works were located. (Andrew S. Mason)

1

Beginnings

The North Staffordshire Railway was borne out of the railway mania of the 1840s, but there had been railways since the late eighteenth century. Probably the first was the wagonway built by the Trent & Mersey Canal, which was authorised on 13 May 1776 to run from limestone quarries at Caldon Low down to the canal basin 649 feet (198 metres) below at Froghall. This 4-mile line was opened in 1777/8 and used wooden rails topped with strips of cast iron at a cost of 20*s* per yard. The wagonway was rebuilt and rerouted in 1785, which did much to even out the ruling gradient and avoid many of the tighter curves of the original line. A new wharf was constructed at Froghall to serve the wagonway, which reduced the distance covered by 500 yards. But even this didn't solve many of the operational problems, so in 1802 the Trent & Mersey Canal obtained an Act of Parliament to build a new wagonway on a different alignment 'to be laid double, on stone blocks, with a moderate and proper slope, with intervening incline planes'. It was engineered by the famous civil engineer John Rennie (1761–1821) and opened in 1804. This was a much more heavily engineered line with level, horse-worked sections divided by self-acting incline planes. The line was laid using short, cast-iron L-shaped tram plates supported on stone blocks. The Caldon Low wagonway was rebuilt for a fourth time by local engineer James Trubshaw when it was relaid with 'edge rail' rather than plate rails. Finally, these early schemes were replaced by a 3-foot 6-inch steam-worked narrow-gauge line.

The Trent & Mersey Canal promoted other early railway schemes. In 1802 it obtained an Act to build three feeder lines to its canal. This Act, however, was probably to legitimise the situation as a scheme to build railways 'from the Canal at Etruria to Shelton, Hanley, and Cobridge, another Railway from the said Canal at Stoke upon Trent to ... Lane End, another ... to the town of Burslem' had been started in September 1800.

The northernmost line at Burslem led from a wharf to St John's Square from whence it was extended via a private colliery railway. The second, at Hanley, and the third – and by far the longest – from Stoke-on-Trent via Fenton to Lane End. These early railways had an immediate impact on businesses in the locality – at Fenton one pottery manufacturer had a branch to the Lane End railway right into their factory. These canal company-owned railways stimulated private railways to join them, and in 1815 the first railway company in North Staffordshire came into existence – the North Staffordshire Railway. It was promoted by wealthy coal masters and quarry owners to run from Consall in the Churnet Valley to join with the Lane End Railway. However, the canal company was opposed to this move, and instead it terminated at Weston Coney. The first section opened in 1817 and it was laid using cast-iron tram plates spiked to stone blocks; examples of such blocks and plate rails from the Consall and Caldon Low wagonways can be seen in the Foxfield Railway Museum. Another early wagonway was the Woodhead Railway, which ran from collieries at Woodhead to the Uttoxeter Canal. Work began sometime before 1810, and a half-share in it was advertised for sale in 1812. Another early railway was that promoted between Newcastle-under-Lyme to the Chester Canal at Nantwich in 1806. In 1847, the Trent & Mersey Canal was purchased by the North Staffordshire Railway, which meant that these early wagonways also became part of the NSR. The Lane End Plateway was the last survivor, remaining as a plateway until closure around 1880.

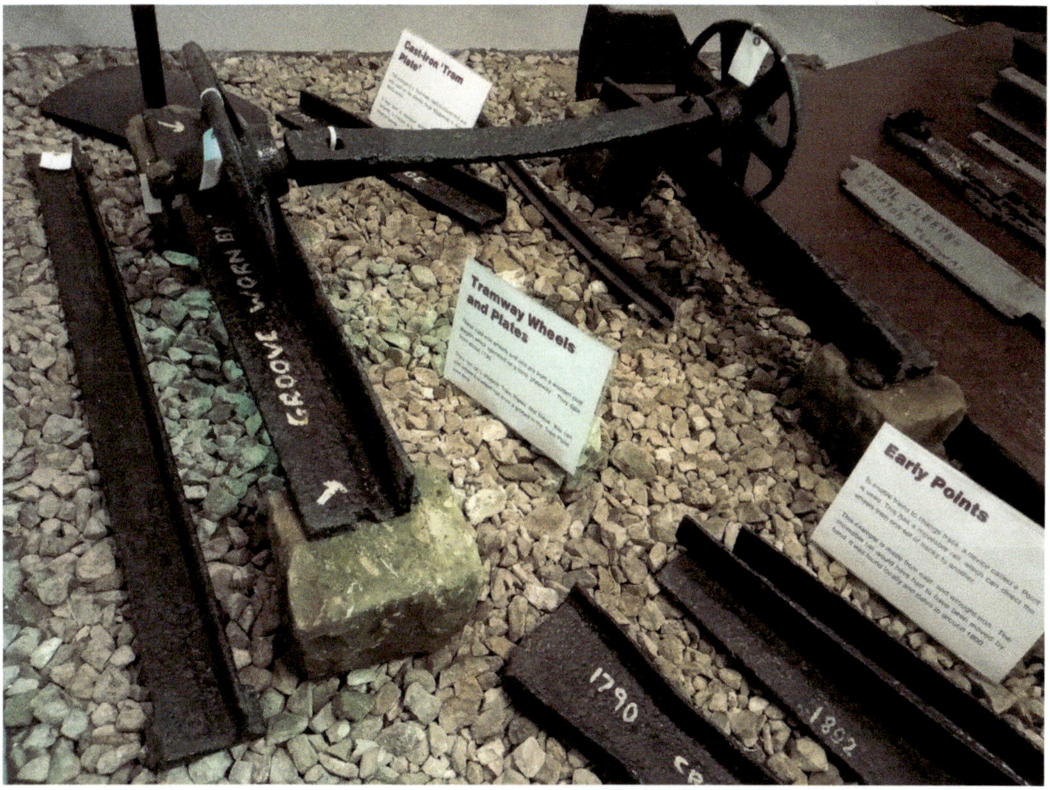

Waggonway components from the Consall, Trubshaw and Caldon Low Plateways on display at the Foxfield Railway Museum. (Anthony Dawson/Foxfield Railway Museum)

The First Mainlines

The first modern mainline railway in North Staffordshire was the Grand Junction Railway, which opened in 1837 between Birmingham and Newton Junction at the midway point of the Liverpool & Manchester Railway. It opened stations at Stafford, Norton Bridge, Whitmore, Madeley and Crewe, and the Potteries immediately benefited from horse omnibuses and stagecoaches operating a feeder service to Newcastle-under-Lyme and Stoke-on-Trent. In the following year, feeder services were advertised as running from Stafford to Uttoxeter, Derby and even Nottingham. Finally, the London & Birmingham Railway was opened, creating much of today's West Coast Mainline in 1838.

But Stoke-on-Trent and its burgeoning pottery, iron and coal industries had been bypassed. The first scheme to put the Potteries on the mainline came in 1835 with the formation of the Potteries Railway. The Potteries Railway was formed on 13 January 1835 at a meeting held in Hanley, under the chairmanship of Robert Edenser Heathcote. Of the resolutions passed at this meeting, one was to approach George Stephenson to survey a route from Harecastle to Norton Bridge, with one branch from Etruria to Heathcote's canal at Newcastle. This scheme met fierce opposition from the canal interest, but its promoters approached the Grand Junction to support it. In turn the GJR carried out its own survey for a line from Whitmore to Etruria to tap into the rich iron and coal mines, and as a concession to the promoters of the Potteries Railway, a crescent-shaped line curving through the Potteries. This, predictably, was not to their liking, so they requested that Stephenson survey an extension for the proposed line from Harecastle to join the GJR at, or near, Crewe. Sadly, this project came to naught in 1837.

Next came two rival schemes to build a route from Manchester, which was both shorter than, and independent of, the GJR. Promoted primarily by wealthy Manchester business owners, these two rival schemes were forced into amalgamation by Parliament in June 1837 as the Manchester & Birmingham Railway, which was planned to run from Manchester London Road (nowadays Manchester Piccadilly) via Stockport, Macclesfield, and Sandbach to Chebsey, 5 miles north-west of Stafford. It thus would have provided the first mainline railway link to the Potteries. Opposition from the GJR, however, meant that the M&B was cut back to join the GJR at Crewe. Opening in stages between 1840 and 1842, opposition by the GJR meant that the Manchester & Birmingham initially terminated at Sandbach, until the GJR backed down, but even then did their utmost to block the M&B.

The Railway Mania

As we have seen there had been various attempts to put the Potteries on the railway map, and the 'Knotty' was born out of not only the various get rich quick schemes of railway mania, but also the fierce rivalry between the London & Birmingham Railway,

Grand Junction and Manchester & Birmingham over control of traffic from London to Manchester. The M&B was the natural rival of the GJR and so formed an uneasy alliance with the L&B, creating a shorter, more direct route from London to Manchester; the two companies merged in February 1845. Into this feud also stepped the Great Western, which, allied with the GJR, in June 1845 threatened to build its own route north to Birmingham, giving the GJR it's desired independent route to London, with the GJR even proposing to relay its entire mainline as dual gauge to allow broad-gauge trains to run into Manchester and Liverpool. To make things even more complicated, the Birmingham & Derby Junction Railway (soon to be part of the Midland) was also seeking an outlet to Manchester. It was in this desire to create new routes to Manchester and Liverpool that the North Staffordshire Railway found its birth.

The 'railway mania' of the early 1840s led to the revival of the 1835 Potteries Railway under the new title of the Staffordshire & Potteries Railway. It covered much of the same ground as the abortive 1835 scheme, but with an additional line from Harecastle to Macclesfield where it met the M&B. At the same time came a proposal for a Churnet Valley line, to run from Macclesfield (M&B) to Derby (Midland) and with a branch from Leek to Stoke to serve the Potteries. The Churnet Valley would therefore have given the industrialists of Manchester an independent route south to Derby, and thence London via the Midland, avoiding the need to run on the tracks of the GJR or L&B. Engineered by Robert Stephenson and Benjamin Cubitt, the Churnet Valley promoters found support for their scheme in the L&B and Midland, but the bill was turned down by Parliament in 1845.

Of the other schemes proposed in the 1840s the most important was the Trent Valley Railway, alias Manchester & Birmingham Extension Railway, which gave the M&B its own independent route south – from Stafford to Rugby. Work started in 1845 and it was completed in 1847.

Having failed to get the Staffordshire & Potteries or Churnet Valley line through Parliament, in 1845 the promoters of the two schemes pooled their resources and in April established the North Staffordshire or Churnet Valley & Trent Junction Railway. John Lewis Ricardo (MP for Stoke-on-Trent) was chairman of the provisional committee. In May 1845, it reached an agreement with the L&B to incorporate their existing Churnet Valley scheme with its own Staffordshire Potteries Railway 'with so much of the Trent Valley Railway as was destined for the service of the Potteries'. The line was to join the M&B at Macclesfield and run via Harecastle into the Potteries 'giving the most ample accommodation to the towns of Tunstall, Burslem, Newcastle-under-Lyme, Hanley, Stoke, Fenton, Longton, and Stone'. It was to join the GJR at Colwich and there would be a branch from Harecastle to Crewe (GJR) and to Norton Bridge, where it also met the GJR. The Churnet Valley line was seen as a direct route from Manchester to Derby and was planned to run via Leek and Cheadle to Uttoxeter. In November 1845, it absorbed the Derby & Crewe Railway, which was planned to run between Derby and Crewe via Uttoxeter and had the support of the GJR.

Liverpool Extension

The GJR was watching these developments with concern. Through its support of the Derby & Crewe Railway the GJR hoped to render null the Churnet Valley scheme through having its own line to Derby. The Derby & Crewe scheme was to run from Derby (Midland) to Crewe (GJR) via Uttoxeter and Stoke, with a branch from Stoke to Colwich (GJR).

The NSR then retaliated, and on 15 July proposed to build a line from at or near Harecastle 'in the direction of Preston Brook or Frodsham, with a view to a direct link with Liverpool or Birkenhead'. Crossing the Mersey, of course, would present a major engineering obstacle. In August, Ricardo suggested the advisability of cooperating with the Chester & Birkenhead Railway over the proposed line to Liverpool, the route of which was via Sandbach, Middlewich and Northwich. Stephenson and Bidder were ordered to survey the Liverpool extension for a Parliamentary Bill to enable its construction. Levels had begun to be taken by October and negotiations were underway for land purchases. Terms were also drawn up with the L&B, as the NSR's Liverpool Extension would have provided them with its own independent route to Liverpool. The NSR thus stood to act as a major crossroads of rail traffic: it provided an independent route from Manchester via Macclesfield to Derby, as well as a potential route to Liverpool.

The GJR therefore sought a compromise, and came to a truce with the L&B. The GJR agreed to withdraw support for the Derby & Crewe so long as the NSR dropped its Liverpool Extension. The Derby & Crewe merged with the NSR in November 1845. They also purchased the Tean & Dove Railway, which had been promoted as rival to the Churnet Valley line, with the support of the Midland and L&B. The purchase price of £13,000 was offset by one-tenth being paid by the Midland and £5,850 by the L&B.

In the meantime, however, the rival GJR, L&B and M&B had come to an uneasy truce. A joint traffic agreement had been signed by all three in September 1845, and from January 1846 the three 'began working as one'. Finally, on 16 August 1846, the mighty London & North Western Railway was formed – the largest joint-stock company in England and a railway that would become a threat to the NSR's existence.

Birth

Finally, after an often-confusing struggle, the North Staffordshire Railway was born on 26 June 1846 following the passage of three Acts to construct a railway from Macclesfield to Colwich (North Staffordshire Railway Act – Potteries Line); from Harecastle to Sandbach (North Staffordshire Railway Act – Harecastle & Sandbach); from North Rode to Burton-upon-Trent, and the line from Crewe to Uttoxeter (North Staffordshire Railway Act – Churnet Valley). The capital was £2.9 million, and seven years were provided for the completion of the railway. John Lewis Ricardo MP (1812–62) was chairman and George Parker Bidder (1806–78), a close friend of Robert Stephenson (1803–59), was appointed as Engineer.

The news of the passage of the three Acts was met with great rejoicing. At Longton a public meeting was held at which 150 persons attended. It was chaired by the chief bailiff (Benjamin S. Brough esq), who welcomed the proposed railway as a great improvement over the 'present inconvenient mode of access, by a Tram Road, to the canal at Stoke' (i.e. the Lane End Plateway). There was however some controversy between the people of Longton and Fenton, given that Fenton would have to wait until the 1860s to get a railway station and it was felt the town would be at a disadvantage compared to Longton.

In order to quash any opposition from the Trent & Mersey Canal, the embryonic NSR took a long-term lease on it. The canal received a guaranteed income and was to be managed by the NSR. Control of the canal represented considerable savings to the NSR: George Parker Bidder estimated that it would reduce the cost of the Churnet Valley line from £25,000 per mile to £13,000, giving a total cost saving of £192,000. The cost of the Harecastle Tunnel would be reduced by £55,000, and another £25,000 was saved by

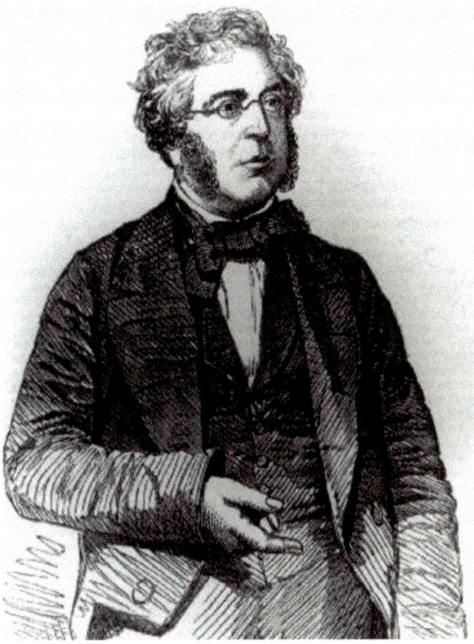

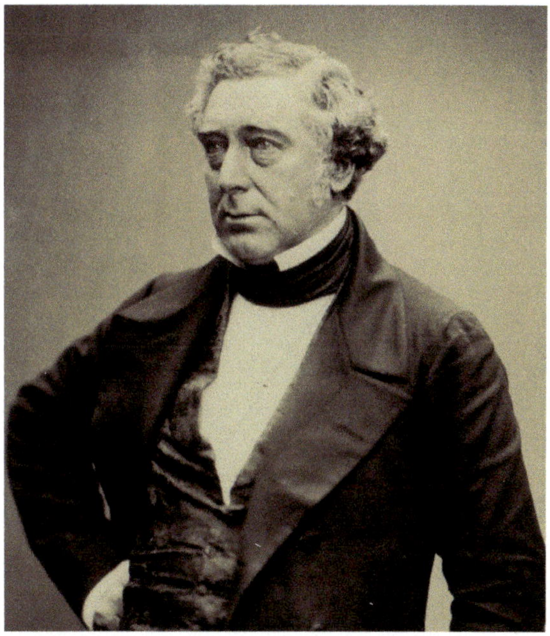

Above left: George Parker Bidder, as a child famed as the 'Calculating Boy' for his skills at complicated mental arithmetic, was the resident engineer of the NSR, representing the chief engineer 'on the ground' to get the line built. (Anthony Dawson)

Above right: Robert Stephenson, builder of the famous *Rocket*, was chief engineer of the 'Knotty' and responsible for the choice of route and selection of the first locomotives. (Anthony Dawson)

being able to build the railway over the canal at any location it desired. Indeed, on the Churnet Valley line the Uttoxeter Canal was almost completely closed – other than the basin at Froghall. Because of this, however, the line had many sharp curves.

Company Officers

The first chairman of the NSR was John Lewis Ricardo, the Liberal MP for Stoke-on-Trent. Born into a Sephardic Jewish family of Portuguese origin, he was the nephew of the economist David Ricardo (1772–1823). He later converted to Unitarianism. He married in 1841 and in the same year was elected MP for Stoke, a seat he held until his death. Ricardo was also the leader of a group of businessmen who purchased the patent rights for Cooke & Wheatstone's electric telegraph, and together with Cooke formed the Electric Telegraph Company in 1846.

The company secretary was Joseph d'Aguila Samuda (1813–85). Like Ricardo, Samuda was a Sephardic Jew of Portuguese origin, and his brother, Jacob (1811–44), married into the Ricardos. Joseph and Jacob set themselves up as shipbuilders and engineers in East London. Samuda was also a proponent of the ill-fated Atmospheric Railway.

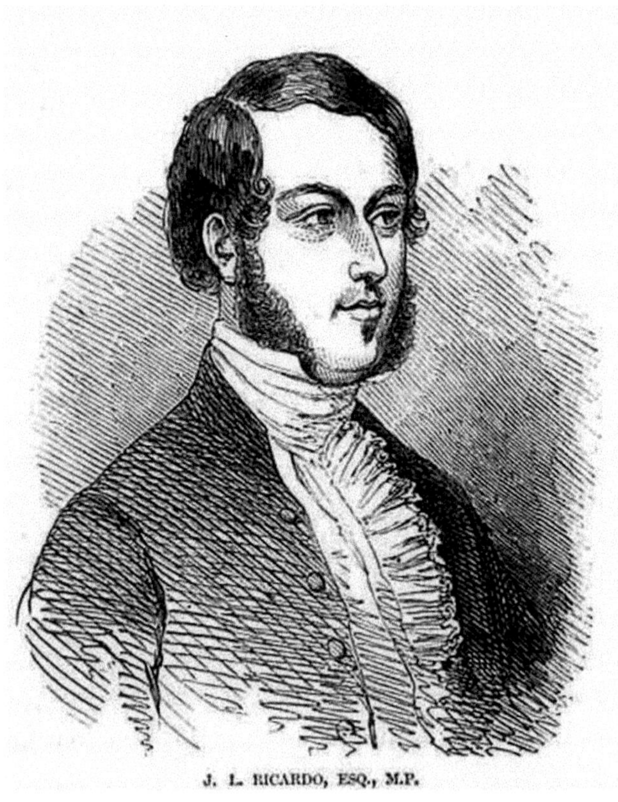

John Lewis Ricardo MP for Stoke-on-Trent and first chairman of the NSR. (Anthony Dawson)

Robert Stephenson was appointed by the NSR's chief engineer, assisted by his close friend George Parker Bidder, the 'resident engineer'. Robert was the only son of George Stephenson and had established the first purpose-built locomotive factory (Robert Stephenson & Co.) in Newcastle-upon-Tyne in 1823. He designed and entered *Rocket* into the famous Rainhill Trials and was responsible for the *Planet, Patentee* and *Long Boiler* designs. As a child George Parker Bidder has been known as the 'calculating boy' due to his ability at mental arithmetic. He made the acquaintance of Robert Stephenson while Robert was at the University of Edinburgh, and in 1834 was offered a job by Stephenson working on the London & Birmingham Railway before going on to engineer the NSR, the London & Brighton Railway, and also railways in Norway and Denmark. His brother, Samuel Parker Bidder (1811–72), was appointed as his assistant. Samuel was appointed as the NSR's first manager in 1848 but resigned in 1853 and went to Canada. He was succeeded as manager by John Curphey Forsyth (1815–79) who also became resident engineer at the same time. He would remain as manager until 1863 and resident engineer until 1865.

Forsyth came from a family steeped in the railways. His father, John (1783–1844), had been trained by George Stephenson. He had been involved with the construction of the Liverpool & Manchester Railway and was later employed as a bookkeeper in the locomotive department. Tragically he was struck and killed by a locomotive on the L&M line from Salford to Manchester Victoria on a foggy 30 December 1844. One son, Thomas, had been riding on the tender of the locomotive that killed him. John and Thomas had both been returning home in order to attend the funeral of a daughter/sister that very afternoon. Another daughter had died in a fire nearly twelve months before.

John Forsyth Jr was trained as an engineer by John Dixon (*c.* 1795–1865). He was sub-resident engineer from 1834 for the eastern (Manchester) half of the L&M, assisting Dixon. He left in 1837 to work with Thomas Longridge Gooch on the survey of the Manchester & Leeds Railway on behalf of George Stephenson. He also engineered the link-line between the L&M at Salford to the new Manchester Victoria station (which was jointly operated by the L&M and M&L) 1841–44 and joined G. P. Bidder on the survey of the NSR in 1845. John took on a younger brother, Joseph, as a pupil in 1857, who acted as his assistant on the NSR. Joseph would engineer the Cheadle Railway (see Chapter 2).

Thomas Forsyth (1820–58) had been taken on at the Ordsall Lane Engine Shops of the L&M in December 1833. Sadly, he lost a leg in an accident when he was run over by a locomotive. Fitted with a cork leg, this disability did not stop him from being the superintendent of the locomotive department of the L&M. He also designed and patented a form of colour-light signaling, which was trialed on the L&M in 1845–46. He also patented type of railway wheel in 1848 and was subsequently manager of the Atlas Foundry of Sharp, Roberts & Co., where he was killed in a boiler explosion in July 1858.

Ceremonial Start

The first sod was ceremonially cut in a somewhat farcical ceremony by Ricardo on Wednesday 23 September 1846. In the morning the first general meeting of the new company was held, followed by a grand dinner where several toasts were drunk. There was a grand procession accompanied by brass bands and various friendly societies, including the Odd Fellows in full regalia; the Newcastle town cannon; and the local fire brigades proceeded to Whieldon Grove. However, many more attempted to join the procession, and before it had even reached halfway 'it became evident there was a great defect in the arrangements, and that the conductors of the ceremony could not have anticipated such an immense concourse of persons'. Such was the crush that the police had to save many 'from being trodden under foot'. When the procession arrived at the field where the first sod was to be cut, there was a 'total absence of any business arrangements'. In the middle of the field was a solitary flag and a small area cordoned

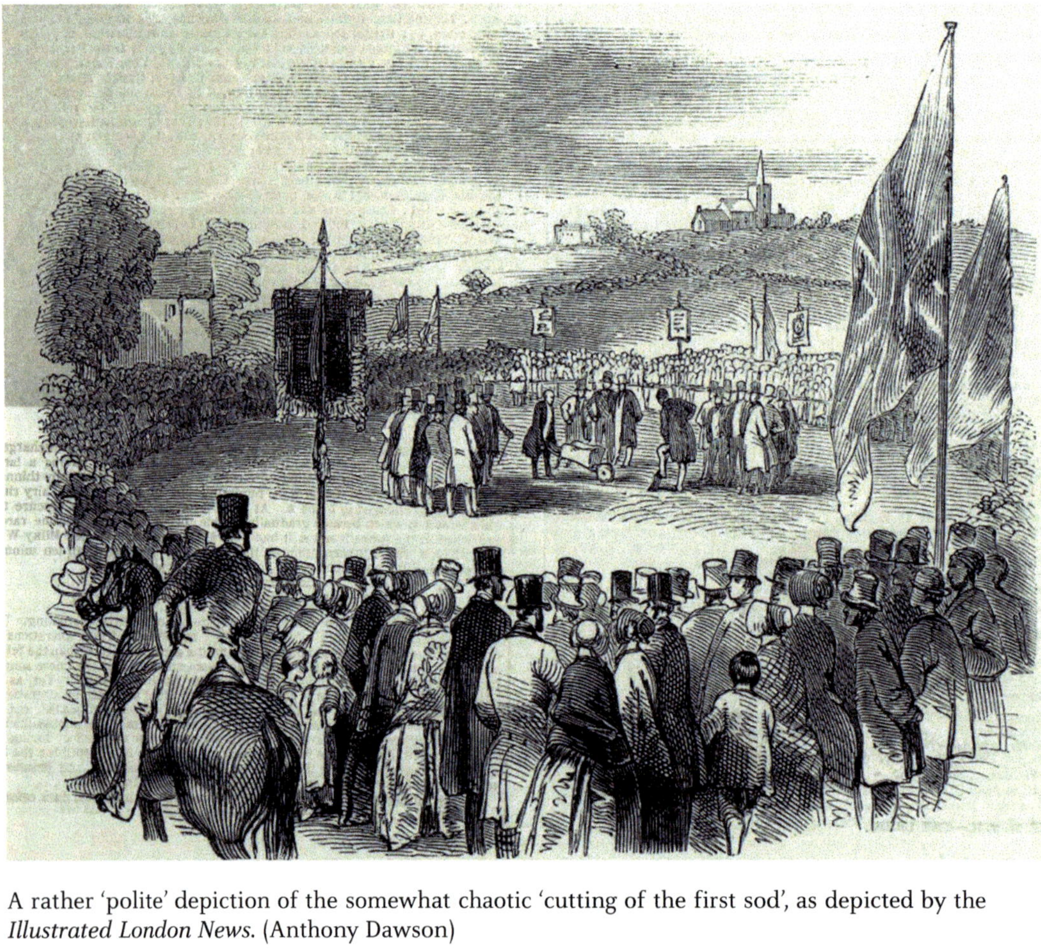

A rather 'polite' depiction of the somewhat chaotic 'cutting of the first sod', as depicted by the *Illustrated London News.* (Anthony Dawson)

off by ropes and guarded by policemen. There was no 'platform or accommodation for the directors, or reporters' and there was no protection from any inclemency of weather, or any seats for the ladies. Such was the crowd of spectators that they pushed past the few policemen and the rope barrier leading to an:

> indescribable scene of confusion. Lords, M.P.s., Navvies, reporters, magistrates, were all speedily huddled together, and a crushing such as I have never before witnessed took place. Many persons were knocked down, hats were flying in all directions, among which was that of Mr Ricardo.
>
> (*Morning Herald*, 26 September 1846)

It was a bedraggled and hatless Ricardo who, in the midst of this chaos, attempted to cut the first sod. The ceremonial spade and barrow were extremely ornate, which only added to the farce. The spade:

> though so beautiful in appearance ... was not calculated for rough usage, and the first thrust of the foot fairly doubled it up and it was with some difficulty that the first sod was cut.
>
> (*Staffordshire Advertiser*, 26 September 1846).

A hatless Ricardo made his way off the field on horseback, the bent spade carried over his shoulder! The proceedings ended with public dinners at the Talbot Inn and the Old Swan Inn in Stoke. In the evening was a fireworks display and a ball in the Assembly Rooms of Stoke Town Hall. The press estimated that around 50,000 had gathered to witness the ceremony.

Construction and Opening

Construction of the line was let in three, later six, major contracts:

1. Macclesfield to Colwich via Stoke, including the branches to Newcastle-under-Lyme, and Norton as well as tunnels at Harecastle and viaducts near Congleton. Let to Thomas Brassey & Co.
2. Harecastle to Crewe, including branch to Sandbach. Let to Mr George Merritt.
3. Stoke-on-Trent to Uttoxeter, including the tunnel at Meir. Let to Messrs Price and Leishman.
4. Uttoxeter to Burton-upon-Trent. Let to Messrs Earle and Combe.
5. North Rode to Uttoxeter (Churnet Valley line). Let to Mr Tredwell.
6. Stoke station and engine house. Let to Mr Jay.

To mark the commencement of actual construction, a lower-key ceremony was held at Stone on 11 February 1847 under the auspices of Thomas Brassey, the contractor. The *Staffordshire Advertiser* reported how all the shops were closed and that 'the local friendly societies and children of the public schools were invited to join in procession'. The organising committee spent liberally on food and drink:

> Measures were also taken to supply one hundred and fifty inmates of the Union Poor-house with roast beef, plum pudding, and ale, – the children belonging to the various public schools of the town - nearly a thousand in number – with plum cake and coffee; while two hundred of the aged and infirm were to be regaled with roast beef, plum pudding, ale, tobacco, and tea, in the National school room. It was also arranged that six public-houses should be opened, at which the navigators and others should be treated with a good dinner.
>
> (*Staffordshire Advertiser,* 13 February 1847)

The first sod was cut and lifted by the Viscount St Vincent, the procession leaving Stone at 12 noon with around 5,000 or 6,000 present. Unlike the near disaster in 1846, things went without a hitch, his lordship cutting and lifting the sod 'in a very creditable manner'. In the evening sixty gentlemen sat down for dinner at the Crown Hotel, at which Viscount St Vincent presided with Revd Gibson Lucas as vice-chair. After no fewer than ten toasts, proceedings broke up around 11 pm. This was followed by a grand ball held on 23 February with nearly 100 persons present. The room had been 'tastefully decorated, and an excellent supper provided by Mrs Wakefield, whose arrangements generally gave great satisfaction'. Music was provided by Worrill's Quadrille Band.

The major engineering work on the line were the viaducts near Congleton and the tunnels at Harecastle. The *Staffordshire Advertiser* waxed lyrical about the tunnel, noting that work was well underway on other parts of the line including the tunnel at Meir:

> The tunnel through Harecastle Hill, on the Pottery line, is an affair of magnitude, and attracts considerable attention ... It will be approached from the south by a cutting of some hundreds yard long, and 70 to 90 feet deep. It will occupy the space between the canal tunnels, but at a greater altitude, being 17 or 18 feet above the water level. In length it will be about 1340 yards, in height 18 feet, and in breadth 25 feet, lined nearly throughout with masonry. To the north will be another deep cutting, and beyond that a short tunnel of about 150 yards long, through the hill beyond Kidsgrove Church. There are now about 500 men and 50 horses employed, everything going on with the regularity of clock-work.
>
> (*Staffordshire Advertiser,* 27 February 1847)

In fact, there were three railway tunnels at Harecastle: north, middle, and south of 130 yards, 180 yards and 1,750 yards, separated by deep cuttings of 350 yards between the north and middle, and 333 yards between the middle and south. Nine shafts were to be sunk along the length of the south tunnel, with six having been sunk by February 1847. In order to carry away the spoil, as well as bricks, etc., in the reverse direction:

> Across the summit of the hill a tramway has been laid for the convenience of materials to and from the various shafts ... The wagons will be worked by the stationary engines [nine in total of 10–14 hp, one per shaft]. Stables, carpenters', and smiths' shops &c. have already been erected.
>
> (*Staffordshire Advertiser*, 27 February 1847)

Despite the progress at Harecastle, work on Meir Tunnel was delayed through water ingress. The *Staffordshire Advertiser* again:

> The works at Meir ... are proceeding with the same vigour as those at Harecastle. The stabling for about forty horses, clerks' offices, carpenters' and smiths' shops, engine-houses &c. ... present the appearance of a village. Four of five shafts are sunk, and powerful steam engines erected ... The water raised from one of the shafts at Meir is of the purest quality, and furnishes an abundant stream to Longton reservoir.
>
> (*Staffordshire Advertiser*, 27 February 1847)

Problems were encountered at Macclesfield, which involved the compulsory purchase and demolition of many houses along the route of the line. Bidder reported in February 1847 that the company had purchased a 'large number' of these which enabled 'the contractor to build forthwith'. There were legal objections to overcome too, such as when the owners of several large mills and a brewery sought an injunction over the NSR demolishing a bridge leading to the brewery and diverting the turnpike leading to Sutton Bridge. The brewery contended that this caused them great inconvenience and injury, but the injunction was refused and instead to be referred as a matter of compensation. By February 1847 some 1,318 men and sixty horses were at work between Macclesfield and Colwich, a number that swelled to 4,000 men and 240 horses by July of the same year. On the Crewe and Sandbach branches the contractor Merrit had 540 men at work and thirty horses, while Price & Leishman on the Stoke–Uttoxeter section had 600 men, 100 horses, 470 barrows and 400 wagons.

By July eight shafts had been sunk at Harecastle and 60 yards of tunnel bricked, while the bricking of Meir Tunnel had just begun. By 1848, 600 yards of the Harecastle tunnel were completed and 35½ miles of single track laid. Some

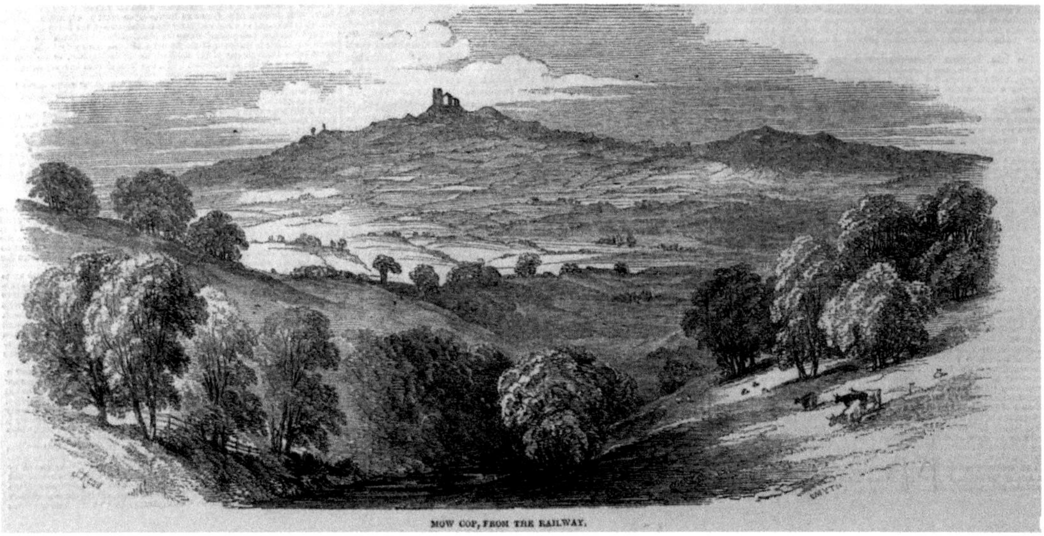

Mow Cop is a village on the Staffordshire–Cheshire border. It was the scene of a great revivalist meeting in 1812 which led to the establishment of the Primitive Methodist Church. Mow Cop Castle, a folly built in 1754, is still a prominent landmark. (Anthony Dawson)

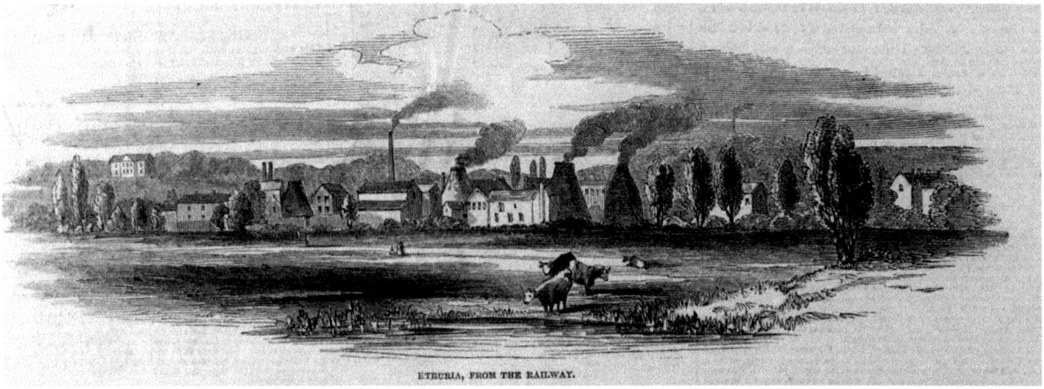

The town of Etruria is still synonymous with that of Josiah Wedgwood, who built his pottery factory there in 1769. He lived nearby in Etruria Hall. (Anthony Dawson)

80 yards of the Harecastle tunnel was yet to be completed by summer 1848. During the excavation of the tunnel it was reported that the navies found 'large fossil trunks of trees (sigilaria)' and elsewhere on the line were stag horns, prehistoric stone tools and Roman pottery. These were donated to the Stoke-on-Trent Athenaeum and Literary and Philosophical Society during the course of 1848 and put on display in January 1849. The scale of operations at Harecastle is shown by the number of horses, plant and equipment put up for sale by Brassey in November 1848: twenty-five wagon and cart horses, six 'powerful steam engines'; and 1,000 contractors' wagons.

Back to Parliament

While purchase of the Trent & Mersey Canal may have removed one major source of opposition to the railway, local landowners would prove far more contentious. Bidder reported to the board that demands of landowners were 'unusually numerous and vexatious ... of a character rarely paralleled, even in railway experience'. There were legal difficulties with Lord Crewe over the Crewe branch, which necessitated the NSR going to Parliament to seek a new Act to get sanction for a 3-mile deviation. Another deviation, 2 miles in length, had been agreed, which reduced construction time considerably thanks to Lord Lichfield agreeing to it running through Shugborough Park. Difficulty was also experienced with Sir Henry Every of Egginton Hall, who would not allow the Marston–Willington Junction section across his land.

The NSR retained consent to build all three deviations under an Act of 2 July 1847. This Act also authorised branches to Apedale, to Lord Granville's ironworks at Etruria, and for an extension of the Newcastle branch to join the private system of Ralph Sneyd at Silverdale. It also authorised the Burslem Loop – not to be confused with the later Potteries Loop Line (see Chapter 2). More importantly, the Act also consolidated the NSR's three early Acts into one. In order to encourage work to proceed at an equal pace, it laid down that no dividend above 5 per cent was to be paid until the Churnet Valley and Willington lines had been opened.

On the Churnet Valley survey work had been delayed through wet weather, and the contract was not let until July 1847 to one Solomon Tredwell. Last to be completed were the viaducts near Congleton. By July 1848 Congleton Viaduct had been completed, and seven of the piers for the twenty-arch North Rode Viaduct had just been completed and the wooden centres for the arches being raised. Tragically, in October 1848 four arches of the viaduct came crashing down. Happily, no one was hurt in the collapse due to 'the workmen being absent at the time'. Seven of the arches were 'completely destroyed. The others are so weakened by the fall that they will have to be taken down and rebuilt' at an estimated cost of £3,000. This 'lamentable occurrence' caused considerable delay of the opening of the line to Macclesfield. The *Illustrated London News* described the completed viaducts in glowing terms:

> The Viaduct at Congleton has ten arches, each fifty feet span, built of brick; the two centre arches are more lofty than any other in England, or even the celebrated Barentin Viaduct on the Rouen and Havre Railway ... The *Dane Viaduct* is the most magnificent feature of the whole line. This viaduct consists of 20 arches, of 50 feet span, divided into three compartments by large bastions ... the extreme length of the viaduct is 418 yards exclusive of the embankments at each end; and the height from the bed of the river to the level of the rails is 106 feet.
>
> (*Illustrated London News*, 16 June 1849 and 23 June 1849)

In January 1848, thoughts turned to opening the first section of the line. It was hoped that the Stoke–Norton Bridge section would open on 1 March and the Stone–Colwich section on 1 May, while the Stoke-Harecastle–Crewe and Uttoxeter – Burton sections would be completed and running by 1 August. Unfortunately, bad spring weather delayed this timetable, and the first section of the line between Stoke and Norton Bridge was opened for goods traffic on 3 April 1848. The official opening was in a grand ceremony on 17 April 1848, from a temporary station at Whieldon Grove from whence the first train departed at 8 am. The *Staffordshire Advertiser* reported that the lineside was thronged from Stoke to Fenton.

The inaugural train was headed by *Dragon* (named after a packhorse of great local fame): 'A compact, active-looking machine, and seems ready to tug away at any quantity of coal.' The carriages were six-wheelers 'divided into four compartments – the two in the middle being for first class, and that at each for second class'. The compartments were 'equally commodious, but the first class are cushioned.' The lining was 'dark blue cloth within a few inches of the top when it is leather.' Each compartment was lit by oil and cost £700 each. The third-class carriages were open, with bench seats, and low sides. Passenger carriages were painted 'claret colour' and emblasoned with the county arms and Staffordshire knot on the door panels. The goods stock was painted red 'conspicuously marked with the Staffordshire knot' in white. The staff wore dark blue uniforms, with silver buttons bearing the Staffordshire knot which was also embroidered on the collars in silver.

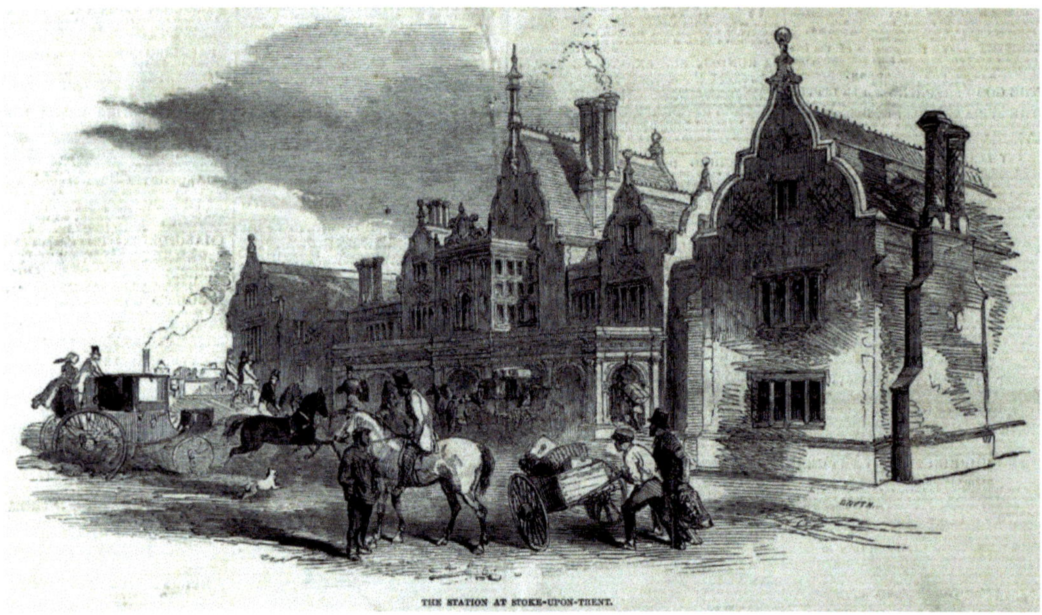

The magnificent station at Stoke-on-Trent was designed by Sir Henry Arthur Hunt of London, who designed similar NSR buildings in the same Jacobean style, including Stone. It opened in October 1848. (Anthony Dawson)

The line from Stoke to Uttoxeter was opened in August. The line was inspected by Captain Simmonds (Inspector of Railways for the Board of Trade) accompanied by Bidder and Forsyth on 3 August 1848. After examining the temporary, wooden, bridge over the market place at Longton and Meir Tunnel he expressed 'his entire approval at their stability' and gave official sanction for the line to open on Monday 7 August. There were three trains each way per day. The onward extension to Burton-upon-Trent would open on 11 September, the combined route being the 'shortest and most direct route between Liverpool and Derby'. The Crewe branch opened on 9 October, when the permanent station at Stoke came into use. The final sections of the NSR system opened in spring 1849 (Stone–Colwich on 1 May) and the major Congleton–Macclesfield section on 18 June with much rejoicing. The whole line 'presented a gay appearance' and the various stations on the line were decorated with flags, bunting and boughs of evergreens. One some of the flags 'the "Staffordshire Knot", somewhat like an ill-made figure of 8, was very conspicuous.' A grand dinner was held at the foot of the Dane Viaduct 'with about 400 guests assembled' alongside the VIPs and local dignitaries. 'About 1,000 of the "navies"', reported the *Illustrated London News*, 'dined on good substantial fare in the open air' and a whole ox, weighing 15 cwt, was roasted.

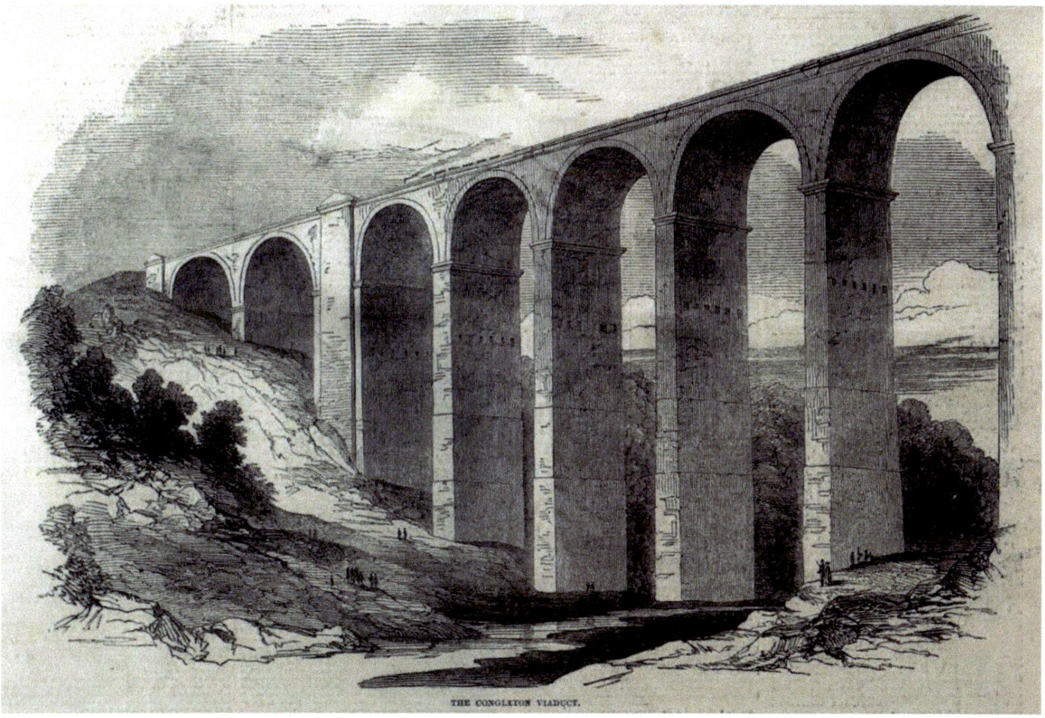

The ten-arch, Grade II listed Congleton Viaduct as depicted by the *Illustrated London News* in June 1849. (Anthony Dawson).

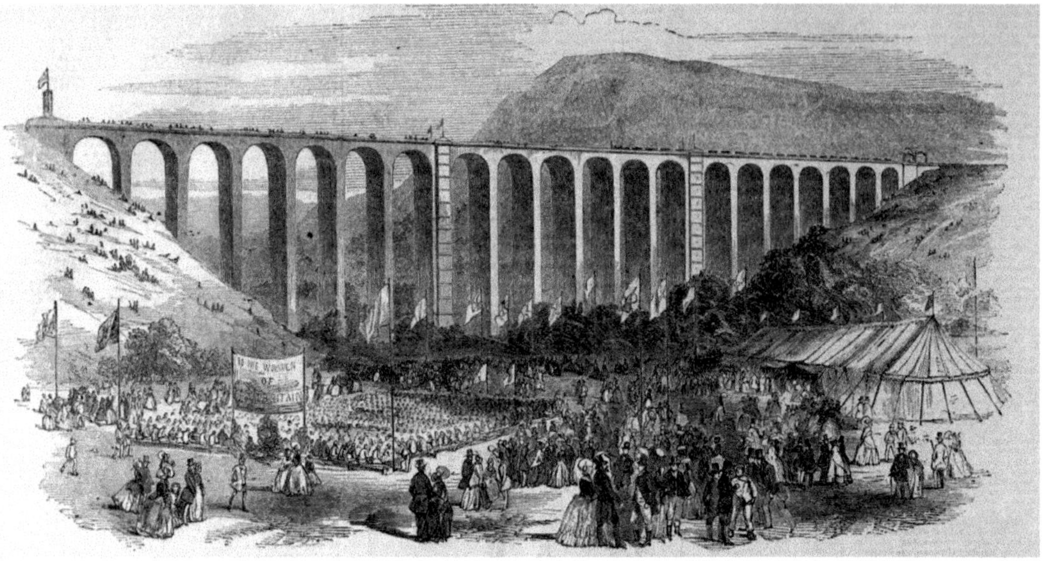

The magnificent North Rode Viaduct was opened in the summer of 1849; its completion was delayed due to the falling of four arches. (Anthony Dawson)

The Churnet Valley opened from North Rode to Uttoxeter on 13 July, along with the 4½-mile branch from Marston to Willington, with the *Staffordshire Advertiser* declaring:

> The North Staffordshire Railway is now complete in all its main features ... and thus the shortest route between Manchester, Derby, and Leicester, as well as between Liverpool and Derby.
>
> (*Staffordshire Advertiser*, 14 July 1849)

The *Staffordshire Advertiser* extolled the natural beauty of the valley: 'Perfectly enchanting ... the river ... rushes wildly over a rocky bed ... thick overhanging woods ... a constant succession of fresh objects before the eye.' It recommended the line to:

> The busy and those who have leisure. The former will be pleased by what they see on each side, as they hurry on their journey, and the latter will not only enjoy the beauties of the way, but will find the roads from any station they may stop at, present fresh objects of attraction.
>
> (*Staffordshire Advertiser*, 14 July 1849)

Twenty-six horses used on the construction of the line were sold at auction in Cheadle and Uttoxeter on the following day.

Operation of the line was leased to Joseph Wright & Sons of Birmingham, a railway carriage manufacturer, for a period of ten years. Unsurprisingly, the rolling stock was purchased from Wright, while the locomotives included six 2-2-2 passenger locomotives built to Sharp, Roberts & Co.'s standard design; twenty-seven Stephenson *Long Boiler* 2-4-0s for passenger working; and ten 0-6-0s for goods trains. Wright was to operate the railway on the following rates:

Passenger locomotives	13*d* per mile run
Goods locomotives	14½*d* per mile run (18 mph)
	13½*d* per mile run (12 mph)
First-class carriages	7/8*d* per mile run
Second-class carriages	5/8*d* per mile run
Third-class carriages	½*d* per mile run
Composite	¾*d* per mile run
Horse boxes and break vans	5/8*d* per mile run
Goods wagons	½*d* per mile run (full)
	¼*d* per mile run (empty)

Wright also had the contract for the maintenance and repair of the permanent way. The NSR now operated 113 miles of double track, forty-three locomotives, 164 carriages and 777 wagons. Everything seemed set for a prosperous future.

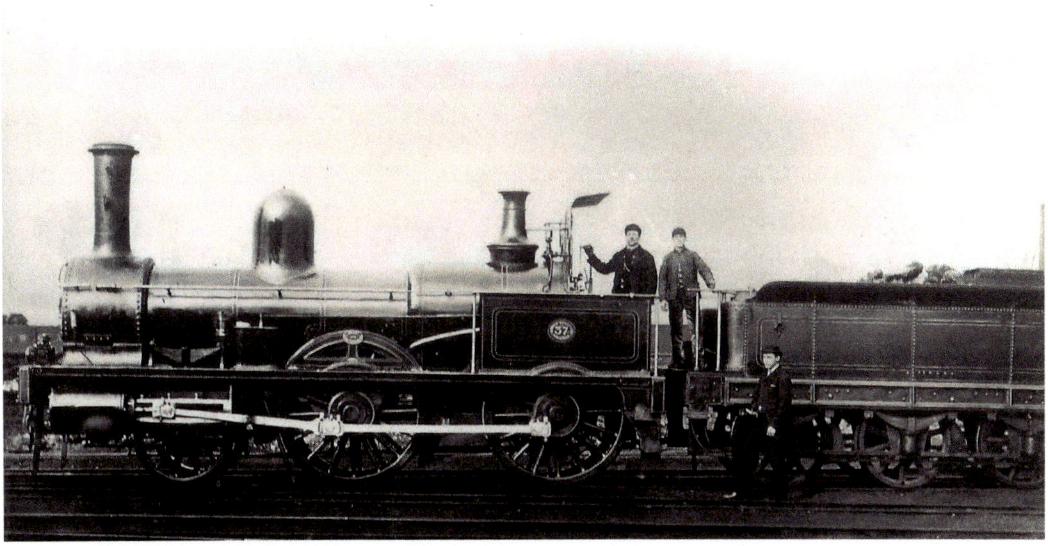

No. 37 was one of the first batch of locomotives built for the NSR, in 1848. Built by Jones & Potts of Newton-le-Willows as No. 42, a 2-4-0 'long boiler' locomotive (all the wheels between the smokebox and firebox). It was rebuilt in 1867 on more conventional lines, renumbered 37 in 1870 and scrapped in 1883. (Anthony Dawson)

2

Fight for Survival and Growth

Almost as soon as the NSR had been created did it come under attack from the powerful LNWR. In May 1846, when the company was only a month old, there were many rumours that the NSR would amalgamate with Euston. To counter this, Ricardo stated at the first half-yearly meeting in September 'as to the amalgamation with the LNWR, I do not see why we should not buy up the L&NWR Railway instead of selling our own'.

The lifeblood of the NSR was as a through route south from Manchester and to Derby in the east. Despite reaching an agreement with the LNWR that every arrangement would be made to facilitate the exchange of traffic:

> It is understood... that the North Staffordshire Railway Company are to have every reasonable facility for transmission of their traffic over the united London and Birmingham, Grand Junction, and Manchester & Birmingham Railway; and that such mentioned companies shall use the North Staffordshire line for the transmission of their direct Manchester traffic; and shall have the like facilities afforded to them... and that any misunderstanding ... shall be left to arbitration.
>
> (Manifold: 39)

Ricardo was confident that the LNWR would uphold their end of the agreement and could not see 'by what pretext either in law or in reason, the agreement can be rendered void'. Sadly, the LNWR did, and the NSR opened legal proceedings against the LNWR in 1849 to 'maintain their right to the whole of the traffic which would naturally pass over their lines between London and Manchester, and Manchester and London'. Furthermore, Bills were deposited for a line from Macclesfield to join the Manchester, Sheffield & Lincolnshire Railway at Marple, and for an extension southward.

Ricardo restated his policy for traffic sharing at the half-yearly meeting on 30 January 1850, stating that the NSR would ultimately obtain the traffic it expected under the 1846 agreement. The proposed link with the MS&L antagonised the LNWR,

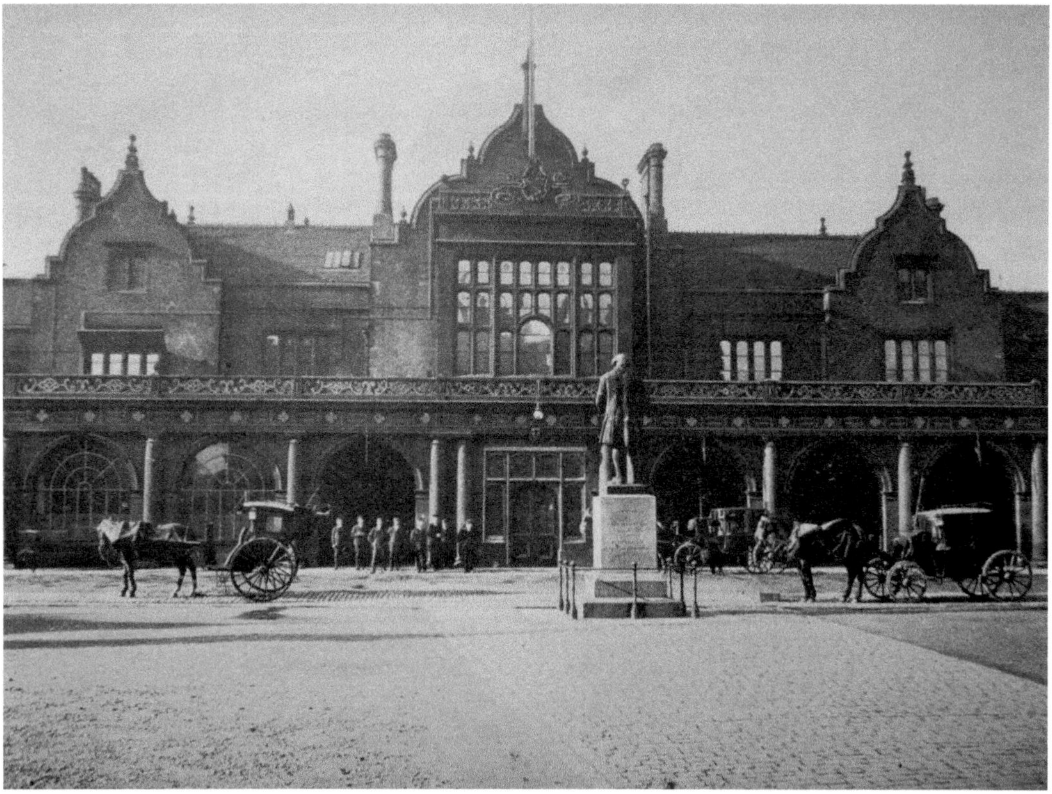

Stoke-on-Trent station as seen from Winton Square, photographed in 1908. The statue, unveiled in 1862, commemorates Josiah Wedgwood. The large window at first-floor level illuminated the NSR Board Room. (Foxfield Railway Museum)

who would have lost traffic from their lines, but also because they were, through an agreement with the Midland and the Lancashire & Yorkshire Railway, trying to keep through traffic off the MS&L. This was because the MS&L and its ally, the Great Northern, represented a threat to its London–Manchester trade. In reply, the LNWR was 'forced to start wooing the MS&L' and ultimately persuaded it to join the Euston Square Confederacy, masterminded by Mark Huish.

This threat of legal action and the proposed link to the MS&L brought the LNWR to the negotiation table in April 1850 and a new agreement was thrashed out, coming into effect on 13 April, but by 1851 the LNWR were apparently beginning to renege on it due to the lack of connections made by the LNWR and Midland at the various meeting points. This led the NSR to look to the Great Western for another outlet by building a line from Colwich to Cannock, as well as to build its own line to Stafford.

Not only was the NSR fighting with the LNWR, but itself. The failure of the board to establish good relations with the LNWR led to a group of militant shareholders demand an inquiry into the NSR's affairs. A committee 'for the purpose of introducing

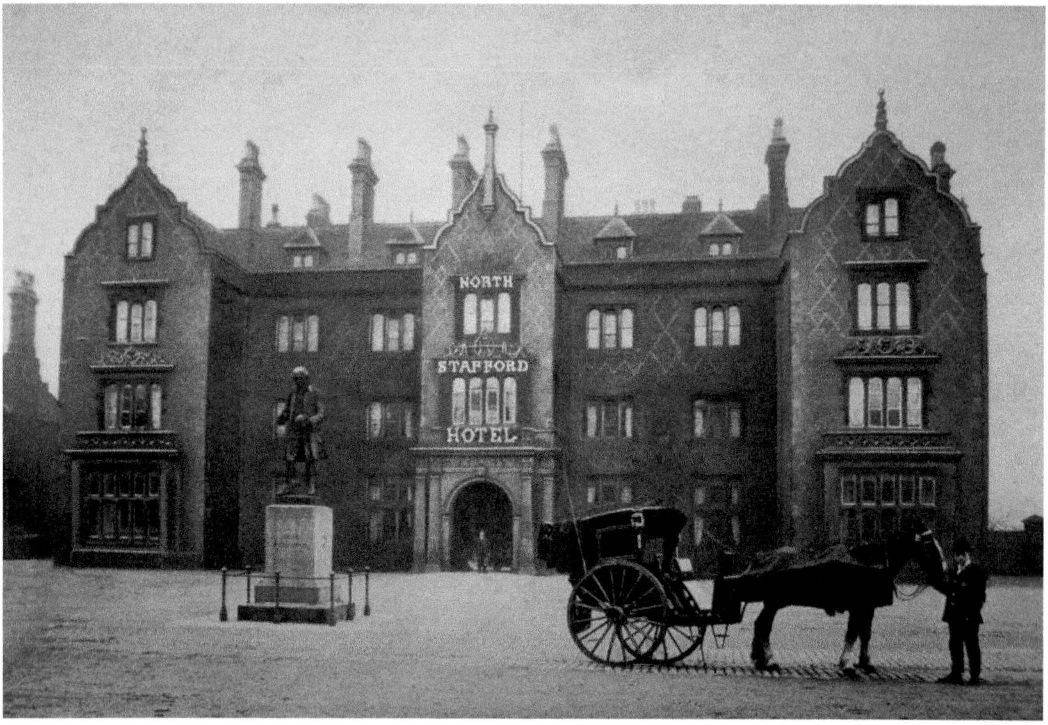

Facing the station is the North Stafford Hotel. It is built in a similar style to the station building and flanked by two rows of cottages, which provided accommodation for senior officials. (Foxfield Railway Museum)

a strict system of economy, and also for a more efficient management' was established in November 1849. Three members – Major General John Briggs (1785–1875) of London, William Challinor (1821–96) of Leek and Mr Taunton of London – were appointed by the committee and three by the directors. The committee believed that nearly £1 million had been spent, which would see little reward. This included £150,000 on the 'elaborate' station, hotel and other buildings at Stoke; the 'useless' branch from Harecastle to Sandbach; the failure to build a line through to Stafford instead of branches to join the LNWR at Colwich and Norton Bridge; and 'the immense sums expended on the engines and carriages, a great portion of which ... are not in use and are daily falling into decay'. The committee also 'regretted the differences' that existed between the NSR and LNWR. They expressed dismay that the NSR had gone to court against the LNWR without consent of the shareholders 'for the acquisition of the London and Manchester Traffic' and had spent too much money in planning lines to thwart the LNWR. Finally, they were upset with how the line had been built with the contract offered to Brassey apparently 'made without competition' and that the contract with Joseph Wright of Birmingham to operate the line for ten years 'ought not to have been entered into without the previous sanction of a general meeting of shareholders'.

A committee of London shareholders was established in January 1850, chaired by Major-General Briggs. General Briggs deplored the 'serious differences' existing between the two companies and that legal proceedings had been entered into by the NSR Board against the LNWR without the consent of the shareholders. Furthermore, he felt the board was biased toward Staffordshire, with no London shareholders being represented.

Alongside the Staffordshire and London committees, one of Manchester-based shareholders was established in March, chaired by E. R. Langworthy, the Mayor of Salford. Like that in London, the Manchester shareholders were keen to get their voices heard. The Manchester meeting resolved that it was 'expedient to appoint a committee possessing the confidence of the shareholders in Manchester' and that any recommendations it produced be adopted by a reconstituted board.

The committee of inquiry were due to meet in London on 1 April 'on the very day' when the NSR met with the LNWR to thrash out new terms. Ricardo felt that the very existence of a committee 'sitting in avowed hostility', one member of which had been in correspondence with the LNWR, had weakened the position of the NSR in negotiating with the LNWR. Despite this Ricardo reported that he had agreed the best terms possible, the traffic agreement coming into effect from 13 April.

The committee still had not reported by summer 1850 and in July two of the appointees, Messrs Heywood and Taunton, declined to put their names to the finished report as it omitted 'certain facts recommendations'. The report recommended cutting the salary of senior managers, including the allowance granted to the directors. The committee also found irregularities in account keeping, with large amounts charged to capital rather than revenue.

There was also trouble with the Midland Railway, but relations were patched up when the NSR threatened to build its own rival stations at Burton-upon-Trent and Derby.

Perhaps the obvious solution to the poor relationship with the LNWR was amalgamation, and three times this was proposed. The first instance was by a Parliamentary Select Committee, which reported against railway amalgamation (1853); the second attempt was barred by the Cardwell Act, which followed on the Parliamentary Select Committee report on railway amalgamation (1854); the third and final attempt was defeated by an alliance of the GWR, MS&L and Midland (1855). Hostilities between the two resumed the following year when the NSR planned a link to reach the GWR (Oxford, Worcester and Wolverhampton) at Wolverhampton, and a third attempt was made to reach Liverpool. The NSR also attempted to take over the Cannock Mineral Railway, but was thwarted at the last minute when the Cannock line joined the LNWR as the LNWR offered slightly better terms (8 per cent compared to 4 ¼ per cent). The NSR had to accept defeat, but a new traffic agreement was reached with the LNWR in 1860, which resulted in further rumours of amalgamation. The two companies began to work even closer from July 1867, with the LNWR being given running powers over the NSR and the NSR able to run over

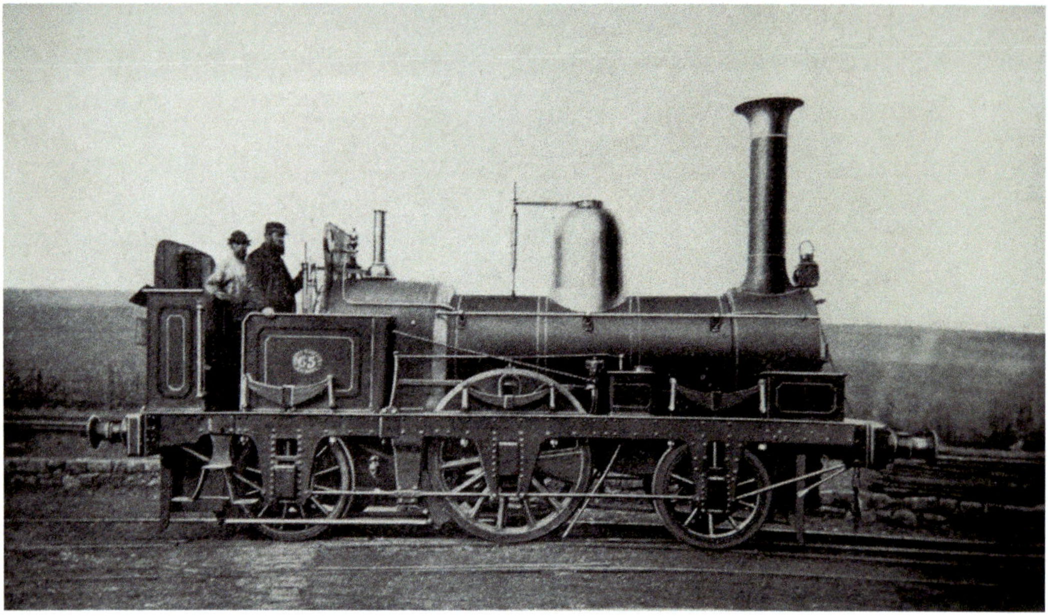

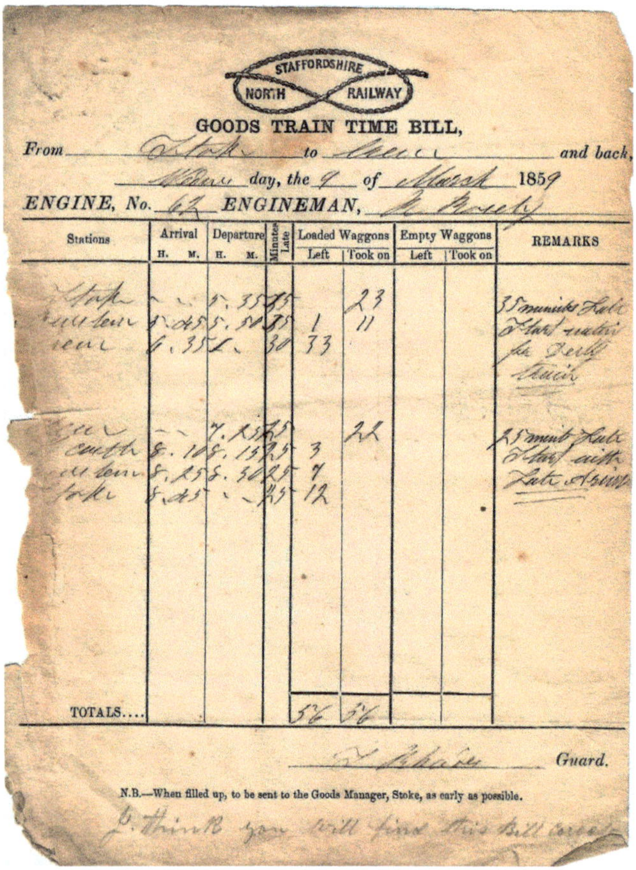

STAFFORDSHIRE NORTH RAILWAY

GOODS TRAIN TIME BILL,

From ____ to ____ and back,

____ day, the ____ of ____ 1859

ENGINE, No. ____ ENGINEMAN, ____

Stations	Arrival H. M.	Departure H. M.	Minutes Late	Loaded Waggons Left	Loaded Waggons Took on	Empty Waggons Left	Empty Waggons Took on	REMARKS
TOTALS....				56	56			

____ Guard.

N.B.—When filled up, to be sent to the Goods Manager, Stoke, as early as possible.

Above: Early locomotives of the NSR were supplied by Robert Stephenson & Co. Locomotive 65 was built by them, perhaps for the Shrewsbury & Birmingham Railway as a 2-2-2 passenger locomotive, but was converted to a well-tank in 1859 and scrapped in 1883. (Foxfield Railway Museum)

Left: This timesheet was kept by Ralph Rosby. He was born in Wallsend, Newcastle-upon-Tyne, in 1830 and was the driver of NSR Locomotive No. 62, an 0-6-0 goods engine built by the Vulcan Foundry in 1855. It was rebuilt as a saddle tank in 1870 and withdrawn in 1885. Ralph Rosby eventually became locomotive inspector at Stoke and died in November 1894. (Foxfield Railway Museum)

the LNWR as far as Manchester, Liverpool and to Birmingham. NSR trains even reached Llandudno in North Wales.

Three further amalgamation attempts deserve to be noted. In November 1875, the MS&L proposed to purchase the NSR – an idea that found favour with the NSR shareholders. Joint working and management was to start at once with the formation of a joint management committee, and there was to be development of an independent route to the south – part of the MS&L's ambition to reach London. After putting the plan to the board, the NSR chairman issued a Parliamentary Notice for amalgamation between the NSR and the LNWR, Midland, Great Northern Railway and MS&L. The terms of the bill were examined and approved by NSR shareholders in January 1876, with the amalgamation to come into effect from 1 January 1877. All proceeded well until the issue of traffic sharing was raised. Upon examination of the financial affairs of the NSR and MS&L it was found the latter was in no stronger condition than the NSR and the bill was withdrawn in May 1876. A year later the NSR shareholders discussed a takeover by the Midland, but this was rejected by the board.

Having consolidated its position with the LNWR, the NSR was now in a position to concentrate on developing its services and expansion. While much ink, time and money had been spent in battling the LNWR for lucrative London–Manchester traffic, the NSR became known as the 'Sixpenny Line'. The NSR proved popular almost immediately, carrying nearly half a million passengers in its first full year (1849). The bulk of passenger traffic, however, was not from the prestigious expresses – through bookings were only a small percentage (11,609). Late in 1849 the board introduced 'closed'

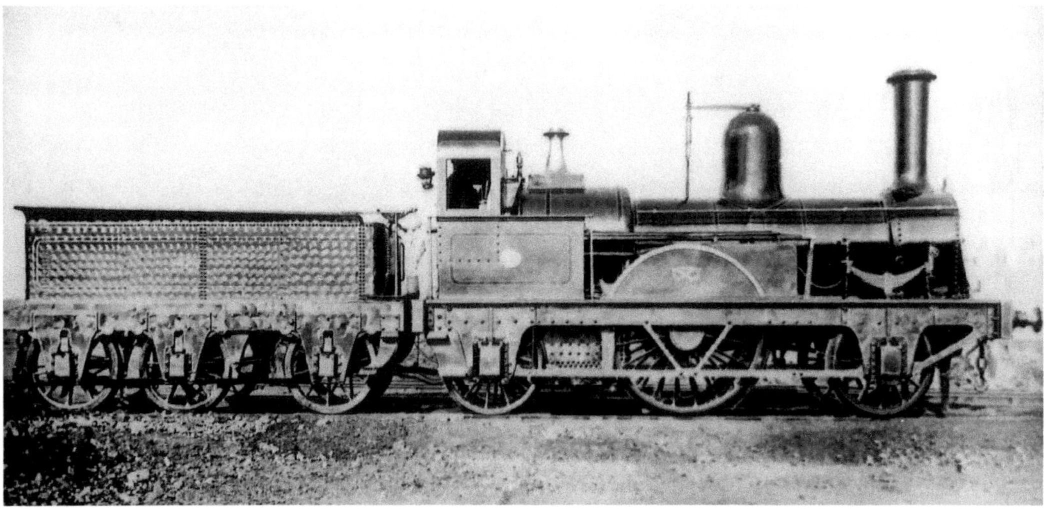

The NSR purchased six 2-4-0 passenger locomotives from Kitson & Co. of Leeds in 1850. They were all rebuilt as 2-2-2s in the following year, and in the 1860s fitted with 6-foot-diameter driving wheels, and later still fitted with cabs. They were withdrawn in the 1880s. (Foxfield Railway Museum)

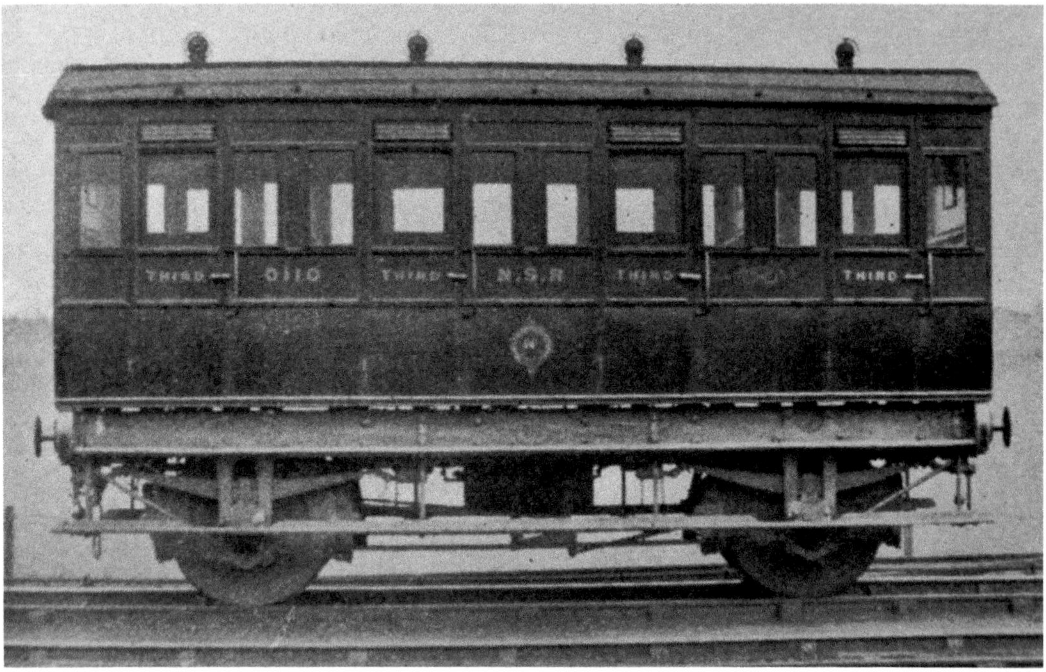

Third-class passengers were the mainstay of the Knotty. Close-coupled four-wheelers like this example were used on the Potteries Loop Line. (Foxfield Railway Museum)

third-class carriages termed 'intermediate' at a rate of 1¼*d* per mile, compared to the statutory 1*d* per mile for third-class travel. They proved immediately popular with passenger returns of September 1850 showing a rise of 22,000 on the previous year. However, it would take until 1852 for all the old, open third-class carriages to be finally converted to enclosed carriages. By 1891 third-class passengers represented 92.5 per cent of the 3.2 million passengers carried in the first half of that year.

Mineral traffic too was booming 'almost beyond the means at disposal of the company for its accommodation'. In 1851, 96,231 tons of goods were carried and 76,092 tons of minerals. The mail was carried from April 1853 – something that the LNWR had jealously reserved for itself, resulting in delays to the delivery of post in the Potteries.

Stoke Works

The core of Stoke Works was the 'monster engine stable', which opened in April 1848 at a cost of £16,750 4*s* 7*d* to a design of H. A. Hunt of London, who also designed Stoke-on-Trent station. This took the form of a brick-built roundhouse, formed from two concentric circles – the outer 200 feet in diameter, and the inner 87 feet. Covering this was a conical roof, topped with a lantern, 45 feet high. The interior was lit via skylights 'running round' each sheet of glass, being 7 feet long. Internally, was a 40-foot turntable and stabling for twenty-four locomotives and their tenders. Around the interior was:

> A 'traveller' ... by means of which the engines can be lifted up or moved at pleasure from one stall to another, for the purpose of repairs while being cleaned.
>
> (*Staffordshire Advertiser*, 22 April 1848)

Close by was a temporary carriage shed, 350 feet long.

Because operation and maintenance of the railway between 1848 and 1859 was under contract to Joseph Wright, the NSR had no need to provide its own locomotive works

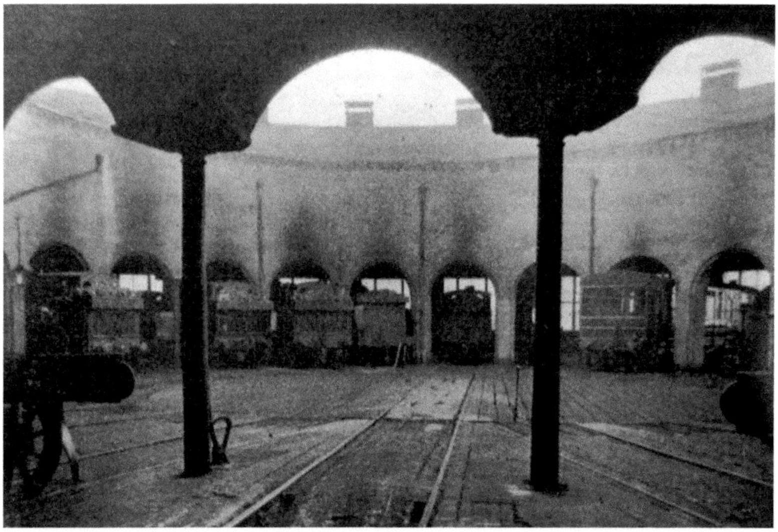

The interior of Stoke-on-Trent roundhouse *c.* 1913 after it had lost its conical roof. The turntable was 40 feet in diameter and there was space for twenty-four locomotives. (Foxfield Railway Museum)

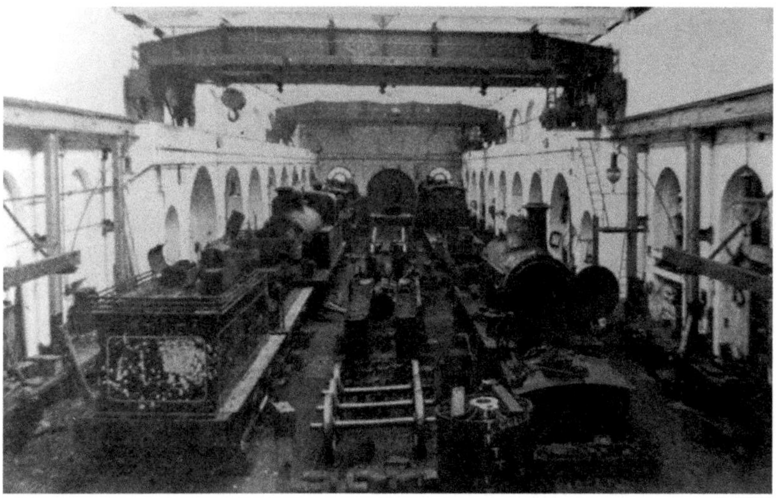

Interior of Stoke Works erecting shop, *c.* 1913. Locomotive construction began in 1868. It was served by two overhead 30-ton Craven electric cranes. (Foxfield Railway Museum)

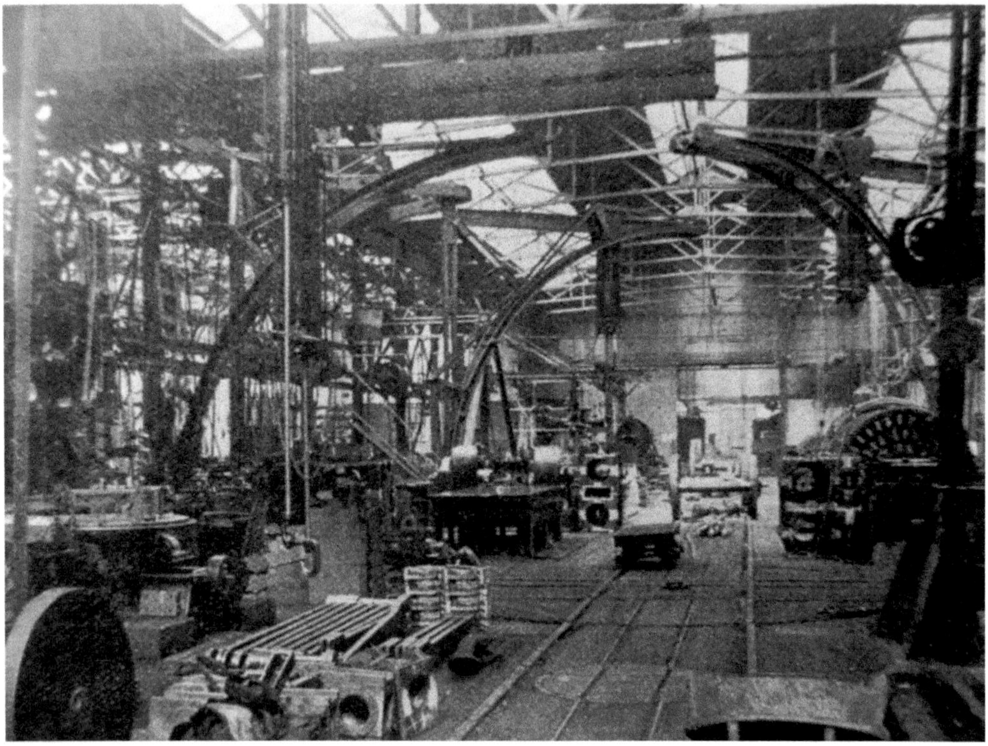

View of the interior of the Machine & Fitting Shop at Stoke Works, photographed in November 1913. (Foxfield Railway Museum)

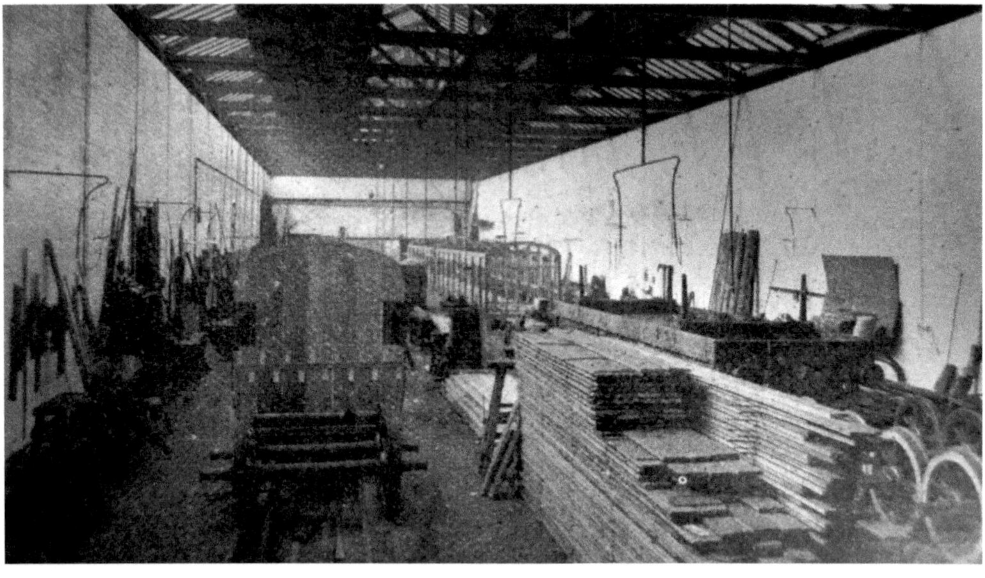

Stoke works not only repaired and built locomotives but carriages and wagons also. Here we see the carriage erecting shop in November 1913. (Foxfield Railway Museum)

or carriage-building facilities. However, the NSR began building its own carriages in Stoke from 1849 and in 1853 provided a small smithy for Wright so long as it did not cost more than £300. Locomotive building rather than simply maintenance began at Stoke in 1866 with the 'rebuilding', virtually as new, of several older locomotives. Two years later the first locomotives were built at Stoke: three 0-6-0 saddle tanks, Nos 5, 13 and 24. Stoke Works became a major employer in the town. By 1913 it covered an area of 12 acres, and 483 men were employed in the locomotive shops and 391 in the carriage and wagon works. The 'outside and running staff' numbered 741.

Until 1874 responsibility for the locomotives was vested in the chief engineer. Beneath them were the locomotive foremen, the first of which was Robert Angus, who had been apprenticed to Bury, Curtis & Kennedy of Liverpool, appointed on 1 September 1847. In 1865, James Johnson, the father of Samuel Waite Johnson of Midland Railway Fame, was appointed as a consultant to renew and modernise the locomotive fleet at Stoke. Angus was left to 'work out the rebuilding details'. Johnson only remained in post for five years until 1870 when he was succeeded by Thomas Weatherburn Dodds, a member of the Dodds family who had worked with George Stephenson sixty years before at Killingworth Colliery. Dodds wasn't destined to remain in post long either due to the acrimonious fall-out resulting from an accident that was caused by his peculiar and patented 'wedge motion', resigning in 1874. The long-suffering Angus was then appointed as locomotive superintendent on 1 April. Angus didn't live long to enjoy his new status as he died in 1875, to be succeeded by Charles Clare, 1875–82. Thereafter the post of NSR locomotive superintendent was enjoyed for twenty years by Luke Longbottom, who introduced a new livery for the NSR, replacing the 1840s

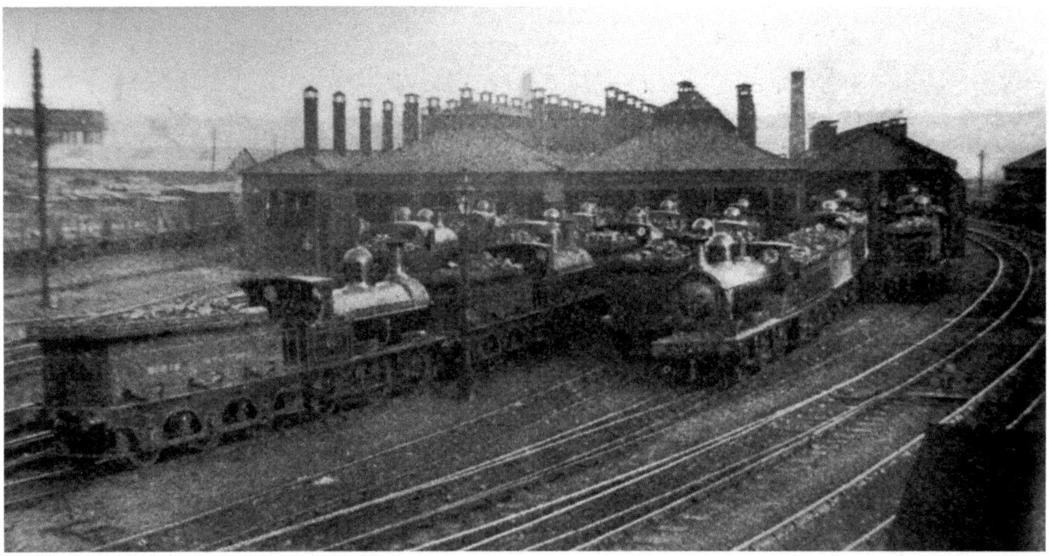

The 'new' straight shed at Stoke as it appeared in November 1913. (Foxfield Railway Museum)

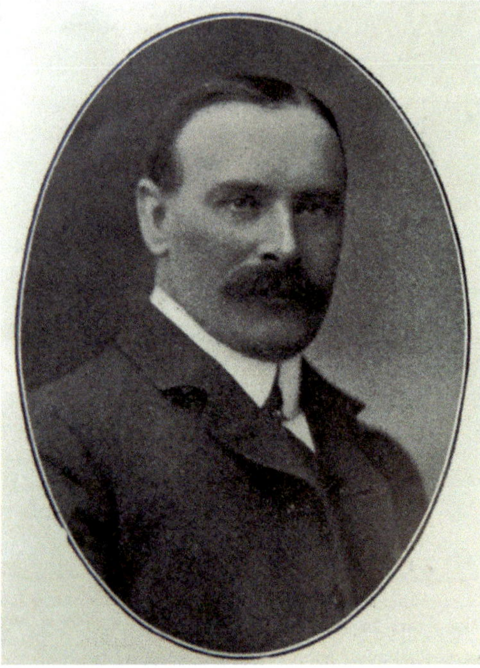 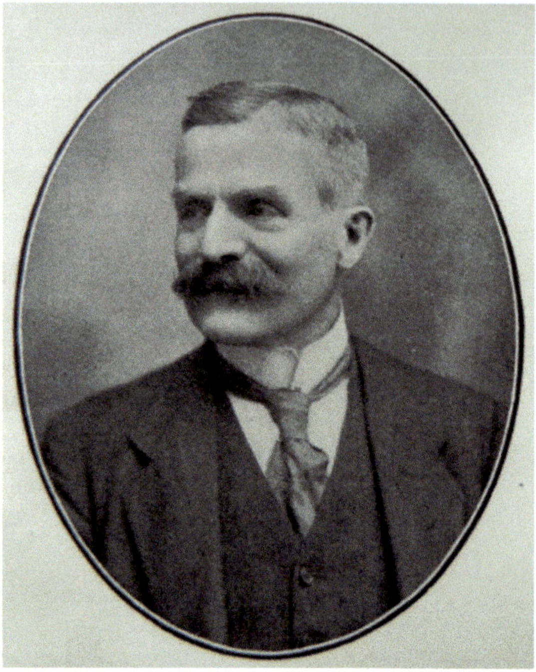

Above left: John Henry Adams (1860–1915) served as NSR locomotive and carriage superintendent from 1902 until his sudden death in 1915. He did much to standardise and modernise the NSR locomotive fleet. (Foxfield Railway Museum)

Above right: John Albert Hookham (1863–1934) was the NSR's final locomotive superintendent 1915–23. Among his innovations was a unique four-cylinder tank locomotive (NSR No. 23) and a four-wheel battery electric locomotive. (Foxfield Railway Museum).

green with 'Victoria Brown' a rich red-brown colour. Longbottom also introduced standard designs and standard boilers, which would be maintained by his successor John Henry Adams. Upon his appointment in April 1902 Adams introduced the famous madder-lake livery, lined in black-edged pale yellow. Adams died unexpectedly in December 1915, replaced by John Albert Hookham.

Branches

Pretty much as soon as the NSR had opened, expansion plans were on the table. A branch from Rocester to Ashbourne was sanctioned by Parliament as early as 1848, and a coach service began running between these two locales when the Churnet Valley line opened in 1849. The first sod for the Ashbourne branch was cut in July 1851 and was constructed by Thomas Brassey, who also had the agreement to work the line for £1,320 per annum. It was formally opened on 31 May 1852. An unusual stipulation in the Act was that the railway was not to pass within 60 yards of Ashbourne parish church, and in 1899 it became a through-route when the LNWR opened its Buxton–Ashbourne line, 'giving a desirable alternative express route from Manchester to London'. A joint station replaced that built by the NSR.

Next came the branch to Newcastle-under-Lyme. Work started on the route in 1849. It was necessary to drive two tunnels (96 yards and 605 yards) at Hartshill, but it was halted in January 1850 due to legal injunctions from local landowners. Thus, the NSR needed extra powers to continue building the branch, which were gained in an Act of 15 July 1850. The line finally opened on 6 September 1852 having cost far above its original estimate. The branch to Newcastle was extended westwards via the private system of Ralph Sneyd, who had extensive ironworks at Silverdale. Sneyd took construction of a rail link to the NSR at Newcastle into his own hands, doubting at the time that the NSR would ever build their own line to Newcastle. He started work in 1850 on a line 2 miles 28 chains long from Pool Dam, known as the Silverdale & Newcastle-under-Lyme Railway. The NSR then agreed to make an end-on junction with the S&NLR at Knutton so long as Sneyd guaranteed to send traffic over the new line. Part of Heathcote's Canal – now obsolete – was filled in and used as part of the course of the railway for quarter of a mile between Newcastle and Brampton. Another part of the canal was filled in to provide space for the goods yard at Newcastle, which

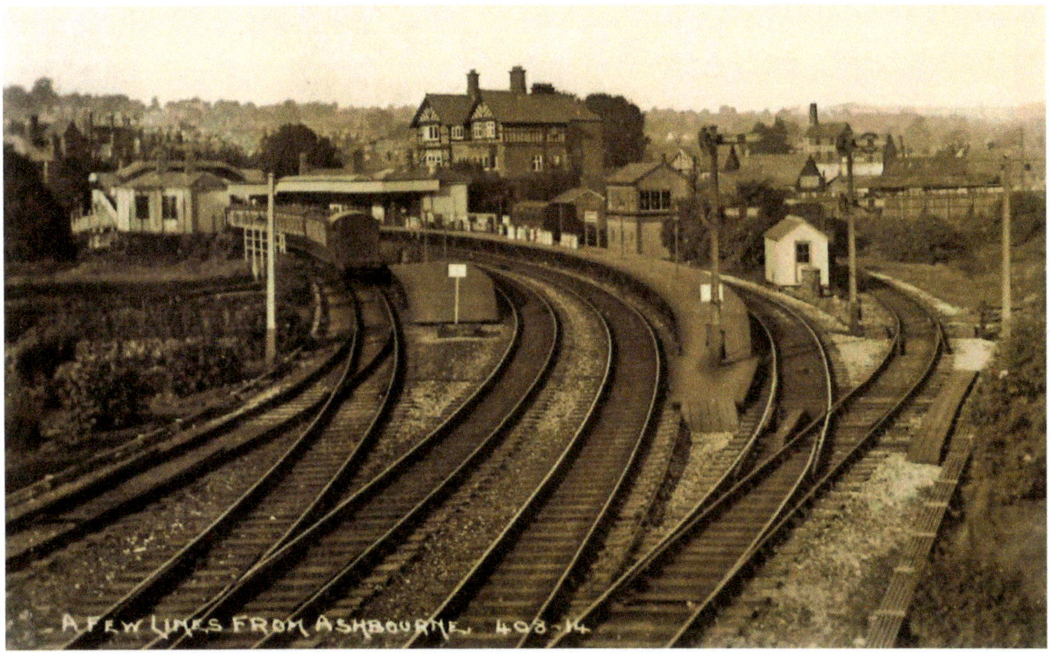

Ashbourne station opened in 1852 on the NSR branch from Rocester on the Churnet Valley Line. The NSR made arrangements with the Midland and LNWR for through traffic to London in the 1880s and 1890s. (Anthony Dawson)

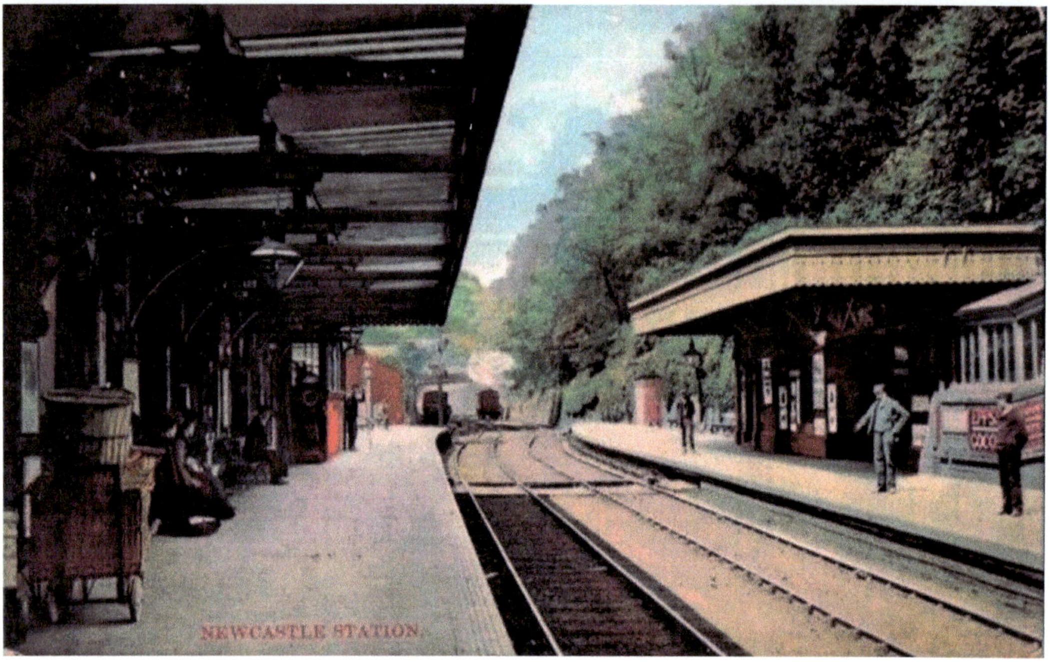

The now-demolished Newcastle-under-Lyne station as it appeared in Edwardian days, *c.* 1910. (Anthony Dawson)

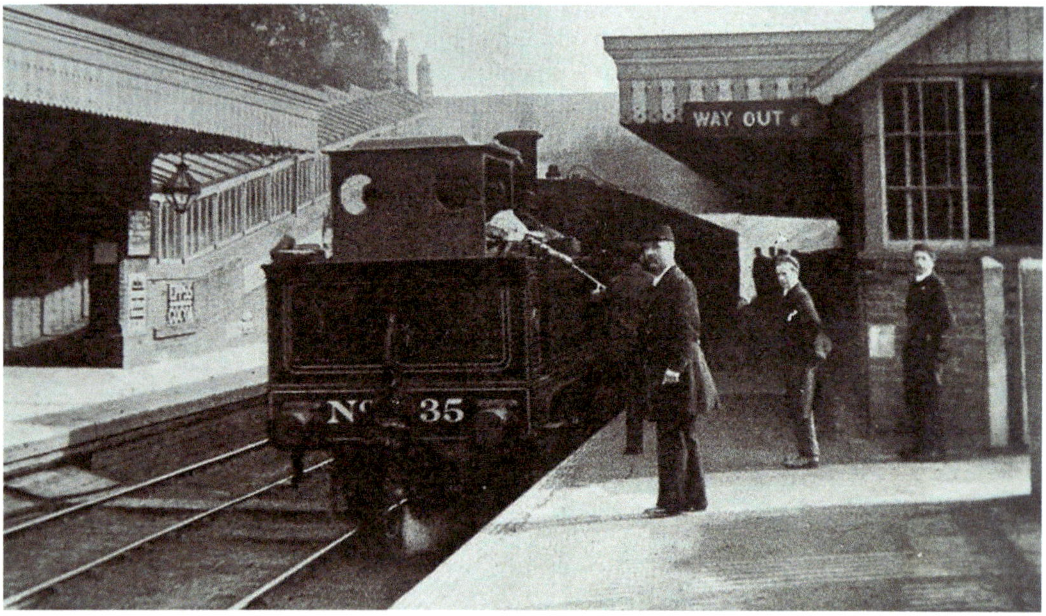

Another view of Newcastle station, *c.* 1890. The locomotive is 'A' Class 2-4-0 passenger tank engine No. 35, built at Stoke in 1881. It was rebuilt in 1898 as a 2-4-2T. It was scrapped in October 1932. (Foxfield Railway Museum)

opened on 7 November 1853. The NSR took out a lease on Sneyd's lines for £1,250 per annum and a further £600 p.a. for the canal on 31 August 1860. In the following year, Sneyd received powers to extend his own Talk o' th' Hill colliery system, the proposed NSR line at Red Street Junction, to serve a coal pit and chemical works at Jamage. He even proposed in 1862 to extend his private line to make a connection with the NSR mainline at Chatterley but this never materialised. In July 1864, the NSR acquired Sneyd's Talke Branch, and at the same time the NSR were authorised to build a line from Silverdale to Alsager (the Audley line) with branches to pits at Jamage and Bignall Hill. The 250-yard Talke–Jammage section was finally completed in 1868. The Red Street–Jammage line was abandoned by the NSR in 1879, while most of the Talke Branch was taken on lease for £1,250 per year.

A branch to connect to Lord Granville's ironworks at Shelton – the famous Shelton Bar – was opened in 1850. A branch to serve John Edensor Heathcote's Apedale Pit was also built, but on the condition that the section of Heathcote's canal east from Apedale to Newcastle be handed over to the NSR within seven days of the railway's completion. The line opened in November 1853. The first section of the branch to Sandbach, where the NSR would join the LNWR, came into use in January 1852 between Lawton Junction and Ettiley Heath. Despite the strategic advantage of the line during the battles with the LNWR in the late 1840s, by the time it was completed in 1858 the goods-only branch had little potential for passenger traffic. Carriage of passengers was finally authorised on 3 July 1893 – thirty-five years after the completion of the line and forty-seven since it was authorised.

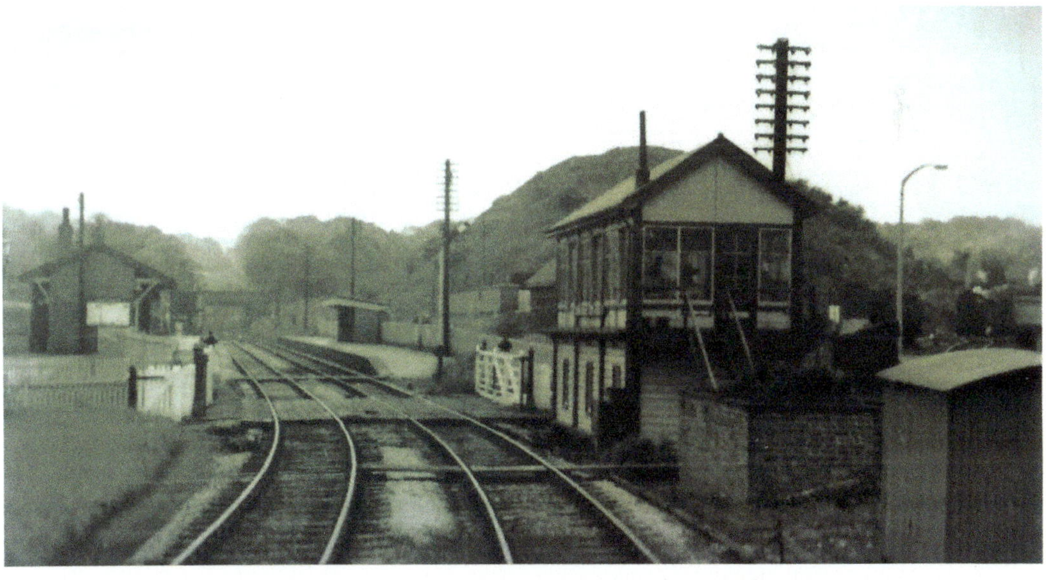

The station at Silverdale opened in 1863 and closed to passengers in 1964. The attractive brick building has been rebuilt at Apedale Heritage Centre. (Anthony Dawson)

The Potteries, Biddulph & Congleton Railway, which primarily served the collieries of the Biddulph Valley, was authorised by Parliament on 24 July 1854, which also included protections for the Macclesfield Canal, which was then owned by the MS&L. Construction, estimated at £20,000, was delayed until 1857 when tenders were invited, the contract going to William and Solomon Tredwell for £87,500. The first sod was ceremonially cut on 27 April 1858 and the board declared the line open on 3 August 1859 in order to meet the Parliamentary deadline. In fact, the line was far from complete, and it would be about a year until coal trains began running on 29 August 1860. The carriage of passengers was delayed until May 1864. The line had been inspected by the Board of Trade in September 1863, which declared the line not safe for passengers. A second report in October came to the same conclusion, despite much protest from the NSR Board.

Market Drayton

The branch to Market Drayton was granted on 29 July 1864. The first railway to reach the town was the 10¾-mile Nantwich & Market Drayton Railway, which had support of the GWR and opened in October 1863. The Wellington & Drayton Railway followed in 1867, having been absorbed by the GWR during construction. Unfortunately, due to

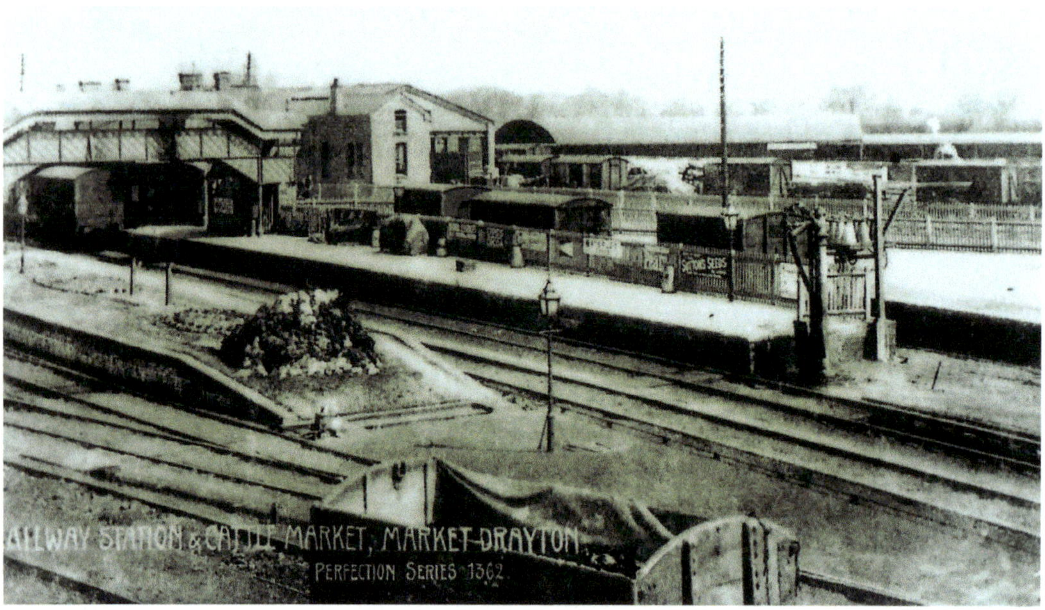

Market Drayton, *c.* 1900 showing the extensive cattle and goods handling facilities. Initially opened as 'Nantwich & Market Drayton' in 1863, the NSR arrived in 1870 when the station was much expanded. It closed to passengers in 1963 and freight in 1967. (Anthony Dawson)

the severe economic depression at the time, the NSR lacked the funds to complete the railway. Although a concession was won from Parliament to delay the completion of the Loop Line (see pages 40 to 42), no concession was granted for the Market Drayton line, which had to be finished in a hurry. It finally opened on 1 February 1870. At first traffic was limited but did include traffic to the racecourse at Keele Park where a station, named Madeley, was opened in November 1870.

Longton, Adderley Green & Bucknall Railway

The LAG&BR was a private railway closely allied to the NSR. The aim was to build a railway linking the Biddulph Valley Line and the Stoke–Uttoxeter line with junctions at Bottleslow and Normacot. The line to run between Longton, Adderley Green and Bucknall was approved by the NSR on 10 May 1866 and received Parliamentary sanction on 16 July. The Act authorised the building of a 4½-mile mineral line from the Biddulph Valley Line at Bucknall to Park Hall. The NSR was to operate and maintain the line. Construction of the line was delayed during the recession of the 1860s and powers had to be extended in 1871. A new Act of 27 July 1872 authorised some deviations to the original scheme to provide a circular route. The new deadline

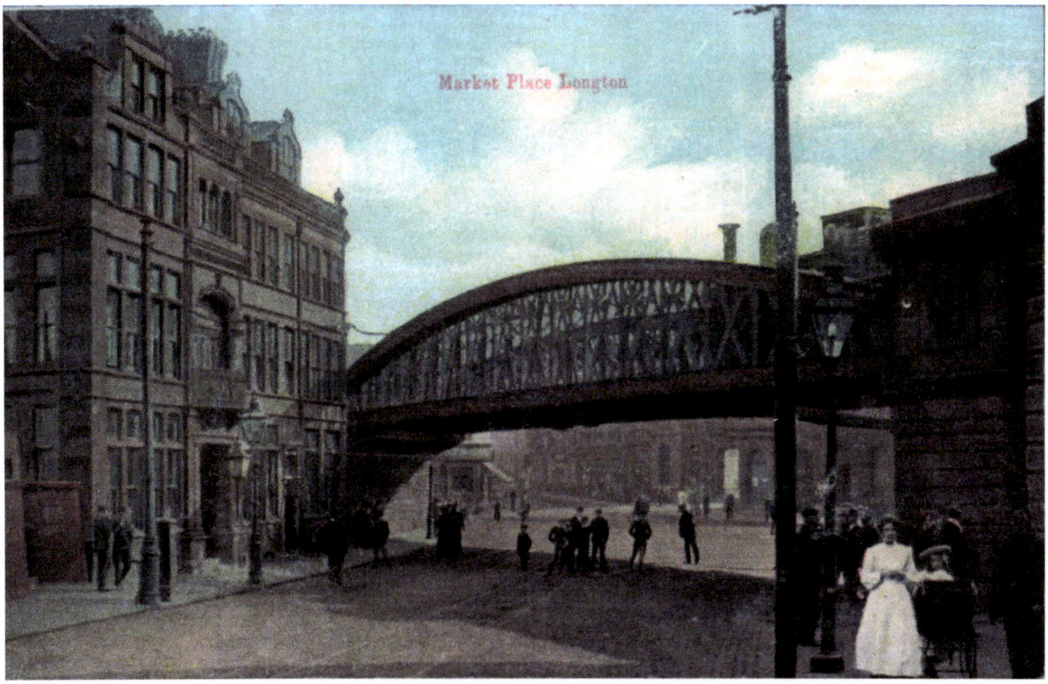

The NSR's line from Crewe to Derby crossed the marketplace at Longton, seen here *c.* 1900. The bridge was completed in 1889, replacing an earlier structure. (Anthony Dawson)

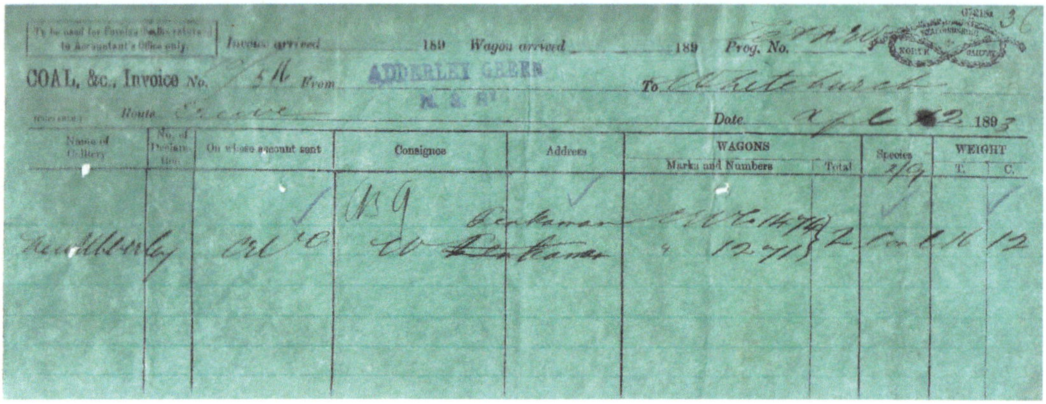

The Longton, Adderley Green & Bucknall Railway was a boon to local coal owners. This NSR coal waybill concerns a shipment of coal from Adderley Green to Crewe in April 1893. (Foxfield Railway Museum)

for completion was 27 June 1874, but this deadline was missed and the line was not opened until 24 September 1875. It soon proved to be an immediate success; in fact it was too successful in carrying mineral traffic. In 1883, it was proposed to cut the line in two, which was carried out when the NSR took over the line on 1 January 1895, with the section between Adderley Green and Weston Coyney being abandoned.

Potteries Loop Line

Perhaps the most famous of all the NSR branches was the Loop Line, running from Etruria to Kidsgrove via Hanley, Longport, Cobridge, Burslem, and Tunstall. A mere 7¾ miles in length because it ran through the heart of the 'six towns', it was one of the most heavily worked sections of the NSR.

The Loop was first envisaged back in 1847, but the idea remained dormant until the late 1850s when the good people of Hanley were agitating for better rail connections. The outcome of this was a branch, authorised on 13 August 1859, for taking over the Pool Dam line and extending the Earl of Granville's private railway into Hanley. The branch was opened just before Christmas in 1861. Initially goods only, passenger services began running on 13 July 1864.

Success of the Hanley branch led to calls from Burslem and Tunstall for their own line. Thus, the Potteries Loop Line was born, receiving royal assent on 5 July 1865. Three years were allowed for completion for the 7¾ miles. However, progress was slow, largely thanks to the trade recession in the UK caused by the American Civil War. Lacking funds and time to complete the line before the Parliamentary deadline of July 1872, the NSR sought powers to abandon the Loop. This was met with fury by the people of Burslem and Tunstall who offered 'the utmost opposition against the iniquitous attempt to deprive the district of the

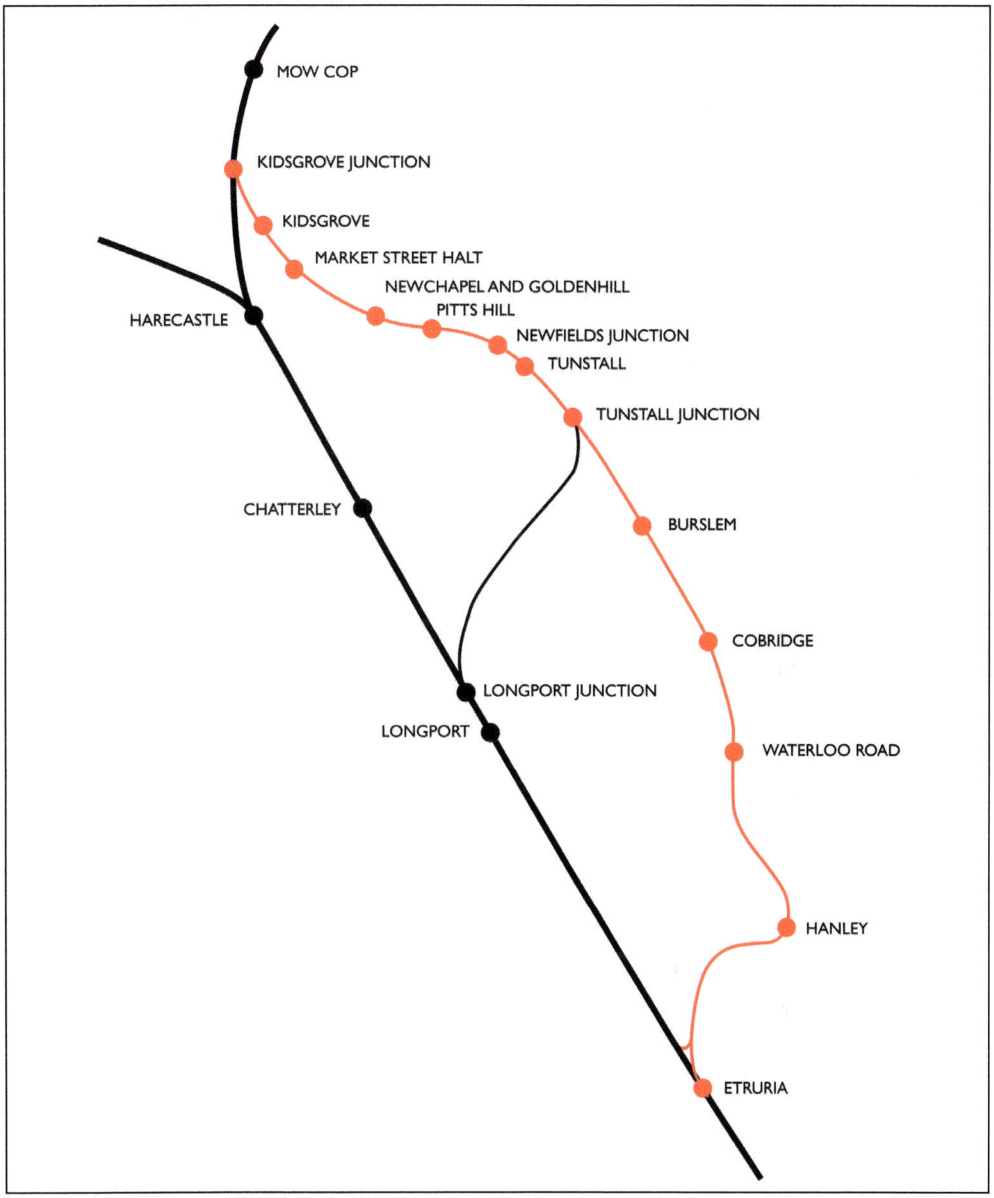

Map of the intensely worked Potteries Loop Line – the Loop Line is coloured in red. (Andrew S. Mason)

railway'. While the NSR shareholders wished to abandon the Loop, Parliament had other ideas and a Commons Committee rejected the abandonment application on 23 March 1870. While progress had stalled, the NSR Board were examining the possibility of building the Loop as a narrow-gauge line to be worked by double-ended patent Fairlie locomotives. The first sod of the Loop extension was cut on 21 July 1870 – the steeply graded route

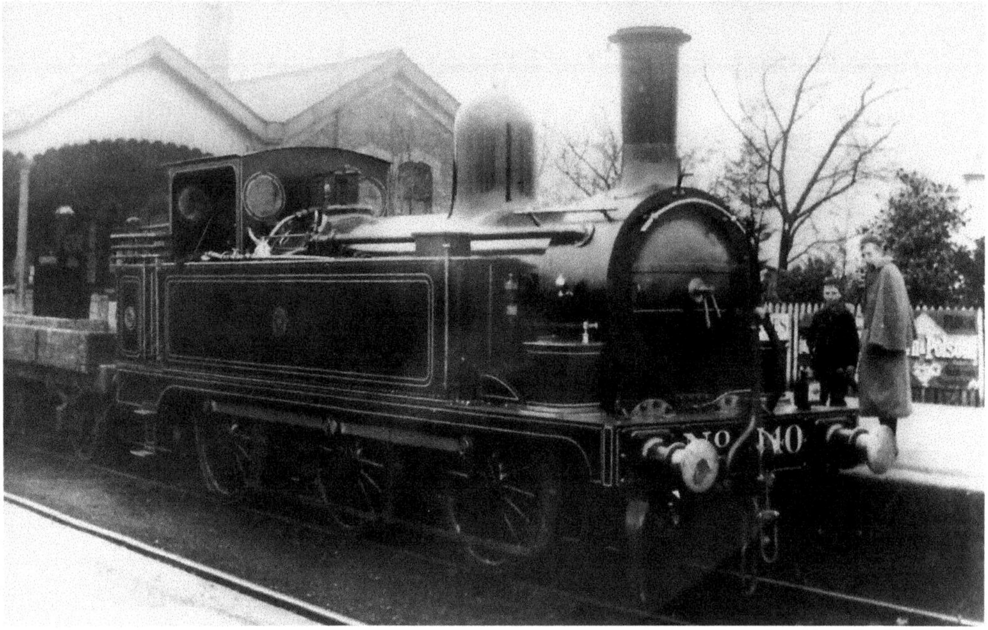

'D' Class locomotive No. 140, built in at Stoke in 1893 by Luke Longbottom. It retains its original open-sided cab and has been provided with vacuum brake fittings. (Foxfield Railway Museum)

required more excavation and tunnelling than any other section of the NSR. The Loop Line reached Burslem on 1 November 1873, Tunstall 1 December 1873, Goldenhill on 1 October 1874 and Kidsgrove on 15 November 1875. The final cost was £493,976 – well above the original estimate of £300,000. The Loop Line was an immediate success. By 1910 there were forty trains a day, using close-coupled stock.

Cheadle Railway

As Allan Baker has described, various attempts were made to bring the railway to Cheadle from the 1850s. With the opening of the Stoke–Uttoxeter line in August 1848, the enterprising Samuel Gosling began running a phaeton from Cresswell station to Tean and Cheadle from 1 September of that year 'for accommodation of persons travelling by the North Staffordshire Railway'.

A scheme proposed in 1878 actually achieved royal assent (22 July) to build a railway from the Stoke–Uttoxeter mainline at Blythe Bridge and run to Cheadle via Dilhorne. Despite local enthusiasm, by 1880 only £37,000 had been subscribed, £10,000 of which came from the Cheadle Colliery Co. Ltd. Following a meeting of the directors on 2 July 1881 it was resolved to wind up the company, and powers were sought to abandon the undertaking in December.

A final attempt was made in 1887 with the formation of the Cheadle Railway, Mineral & Land Co. Ltd. This railway was to again run from Cresswell. In order to avoid the severe gradients of the former Dilhorne route, it approached Cheadle via Totmonslow with a total length of just under 4 miles. Despite Parliamentary approval not being granted until 7 August 1888, the first sod was ceremonially cut on 22 March and work rapidly got underway, presumably on land owned outright by the company. Work had also commenced on sinking shafts of the troublesome Cheadle Tunnel. Everything looked rosy until in December the money ran out; even the engineer Joseph Forsyth (see Chapter 1) hadn't been paid. Work was therefore halted until the winter of 1891.

The first train ran from the NSR at Cresswell to Totmonslow on 7 November 1892 amid much celebration. The line was to be worked by the NSR for £1,240 per year, with the

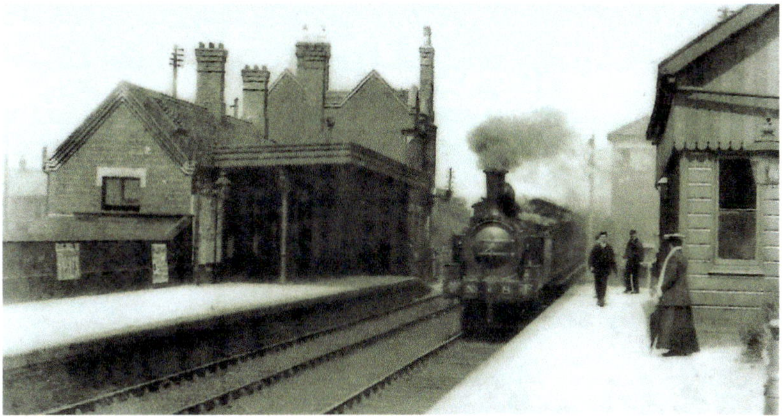

Blythe Bridge on the Crewe–Derby line, *c.* 1890. Running through the station is 'A' Class 2-4-0T No. 8, built at Stoke in 1878. Renumbered 8A in 1911 it was scrapped in 1914. (Foxfield Railway Museum)

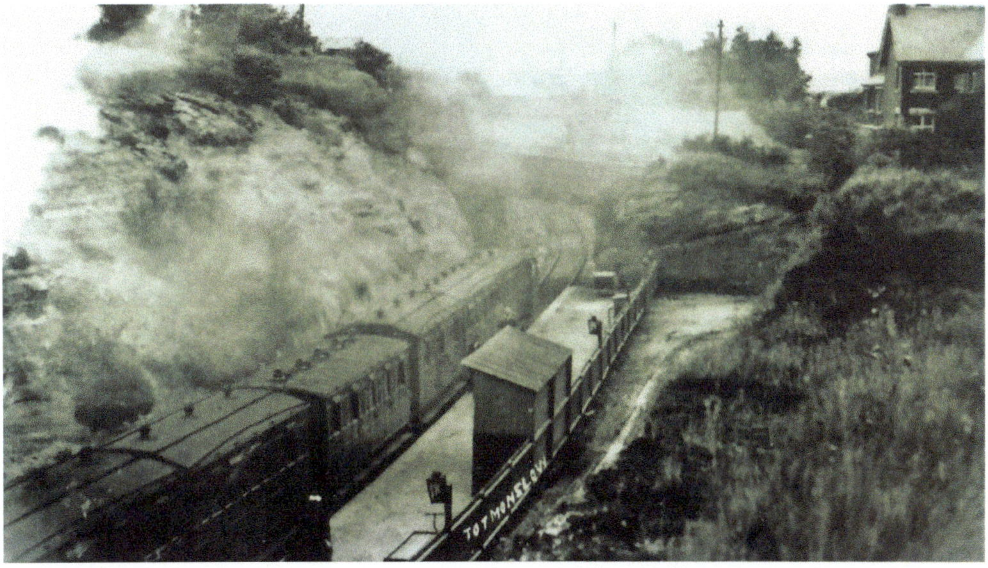

Totmonslow, later Tean, on the Cheadle Branch, opened in November 1892. It would nearly be a decade before Cheadle itself was reached. (Foxfield Railway Museum)

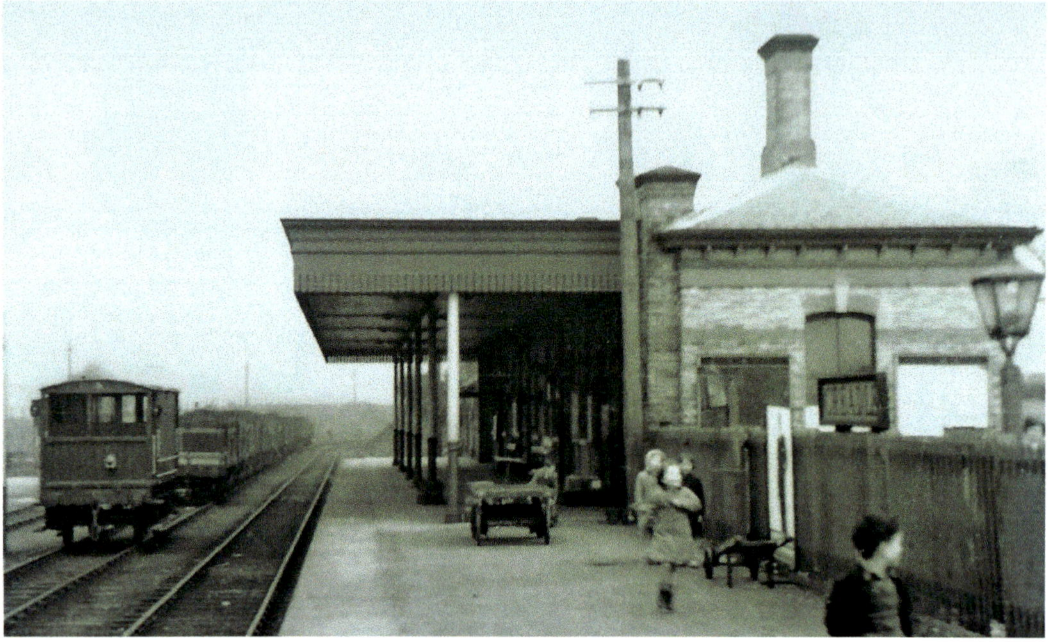

Cheadle, the terminus of the erstwhile Cheadle Railway, *c.* 1950. Cheadle closed to passenger traffic in 1963 although a special was run 28 March 1984 to mark the launch of the InterCity Charter Train Unit. (Foxfield Railway Museum)

Cheadle Railway paying £100 for the use of Cresswell station. It also had to upkeep the permanent way. Any further progress, however, was hampered through lack of funds, and thanks to a new Act (7 August 1896) the Cheadle Railway came into being to complete the line. Due to difficulties with the Cheadle Tunnel, and despite a deviation being authorised, the line wasn't opened to traffic until Tuesday 1 January 1901. Agreement was reached with the NSR to work the line on 25 May 1901, and a year later in August 1902 arrangements were made for the NSR to purchase the Cheadle Railway outright for £50,000, but this was declined by the Cheadle Company. The Cheadle Railway struggled on as an independent company until 1 January 1907 when it was purchased by the NSR, with the Cheadle Company receiving a far worse deal than in 1902, the railway being sold for £39,150.

Macclesfield, Bollington & Marple

The MB&M was born out of the rivalry between the NSR and LNWR, and the former's good relations with the MS&L, which could provide a new outlet for the NSR via the 11-mile branch from Macclesfield to Marple, a route into Manchester independent of the LNWR. It received its Act on 14 July 1864 with the NSR and MS&L providing the joint capital, but again due to the economic depression of the 1860s, progress was

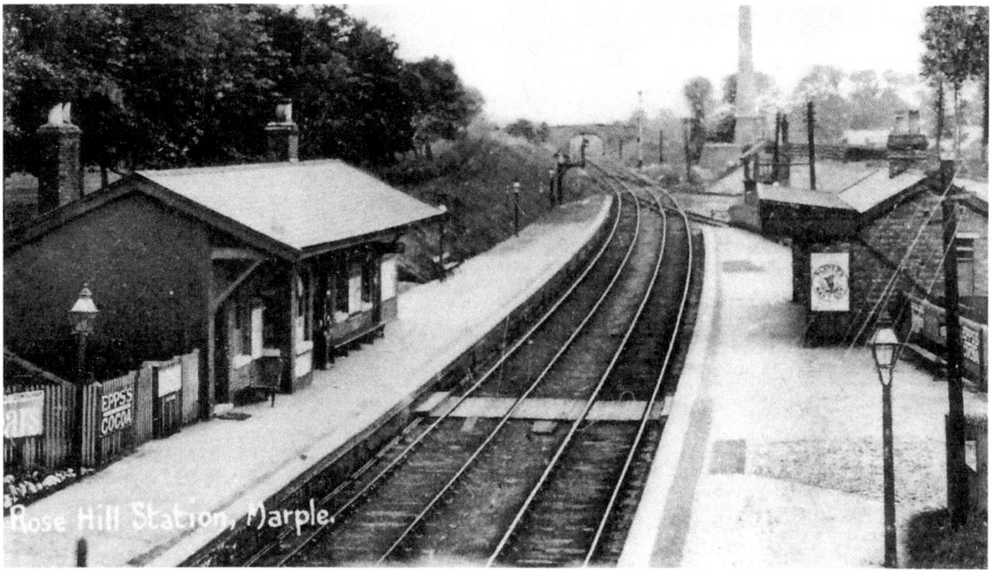

The station at Rose Hill, Marple, was opened by the MB&MR in 1869. The original line from Macclesfield closed in 1970 and is connected by a short branch to the Hope Valley Line. Only one waiting shelter and platform remain. (Anthony Dawson)

painfully slow. The single-track line eventually opened to passengers on 2 August 1869 and to goods on 1 March 1870.

While the LNWR had not opposed construction of the line, it did oppose the construction of a joint station at Macclesfield. Sir Edward Watkin, chair of the MS&L, wanted the LNWR to be a third party in a new station agreement, but the LNWR declined. The situation was further complicated by Macclesfield Town Council, which wanted a new station nearer to the town centre than the existing LNWR/NSR station at Hibel Road.

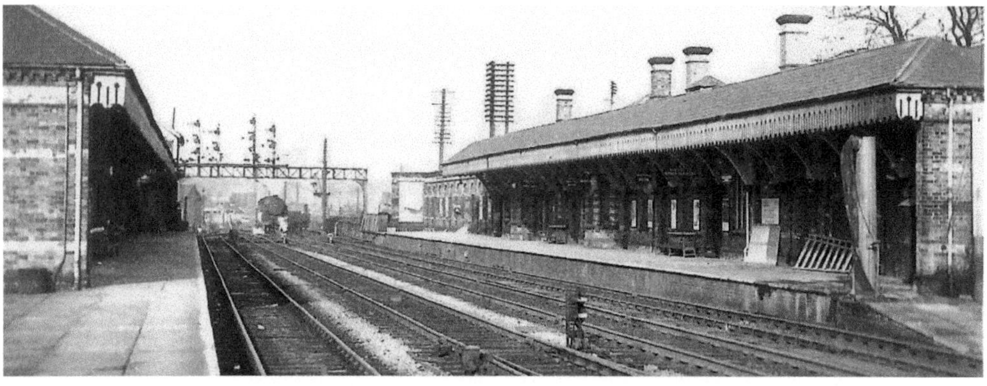

Macclesfield Central in BR days, 1950s. It opened as a joint NSR MS&L venture in 1869–70 and was massively remodelled in 1960 to create the present station. (Anthony Dawson)

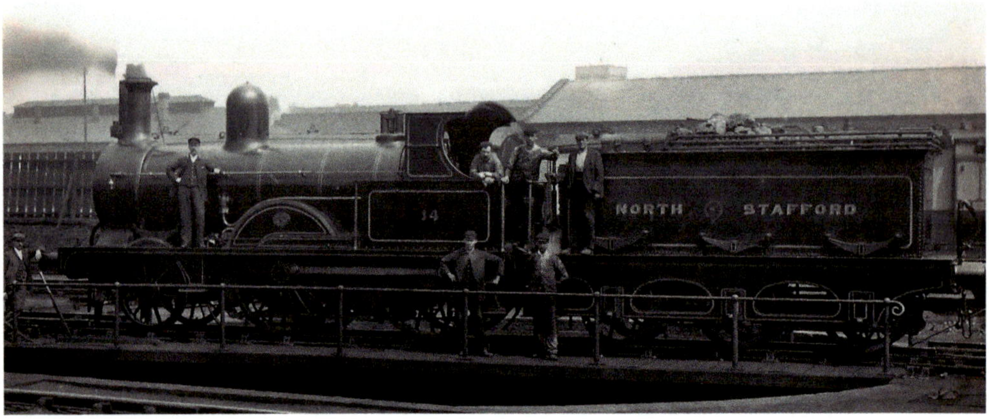

NSR No. 14 on the turntable at Macclesfield Hibel Road. Built by Dubs & Co. of Glasgow in 1875, No. 14 was rebuilt in 1888 and 1903. Placed on the duplicate list as 14A in 1912 it was scrapped in 1919. (Anthony Dawson)

Of the four proposed schemes, the third was a new station – the present Macclesfield Central. At first the MB&M had no direct connection with the NSR until 13 February 1871. An Act of 25 May 1871 brought major changes. The MB&M was dissolved and equally vested in the NSR and MS&L. The second change was the doubling of the line, which was completed on 26 June 1871 and the new joint station opened on 1 July 1873.

Leek & Manifold

The NSR was among the few mainline railways in Britain to also operate narrow-gauge railways. These included the 3-foot-6-inch Caldon Tramway, worked by a pair of Hughes of Loughborough 0-4-0 saddle tanks, and the famous Leek & Manifold Valley Light Railway.

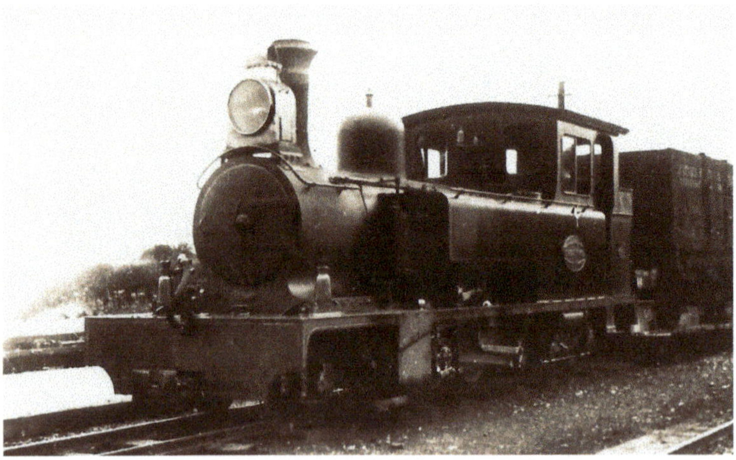

The NSR was unique in running trains to three gauges: standard; 3 feet 6 inches on the Caldon Low tramway; and 2 feet 6 inches on the Leek & Manifold, the handsome locomotives of which were designed by E. R. Calthrop and built by Kitson of Leeds. (Foxfield Railway Museum)

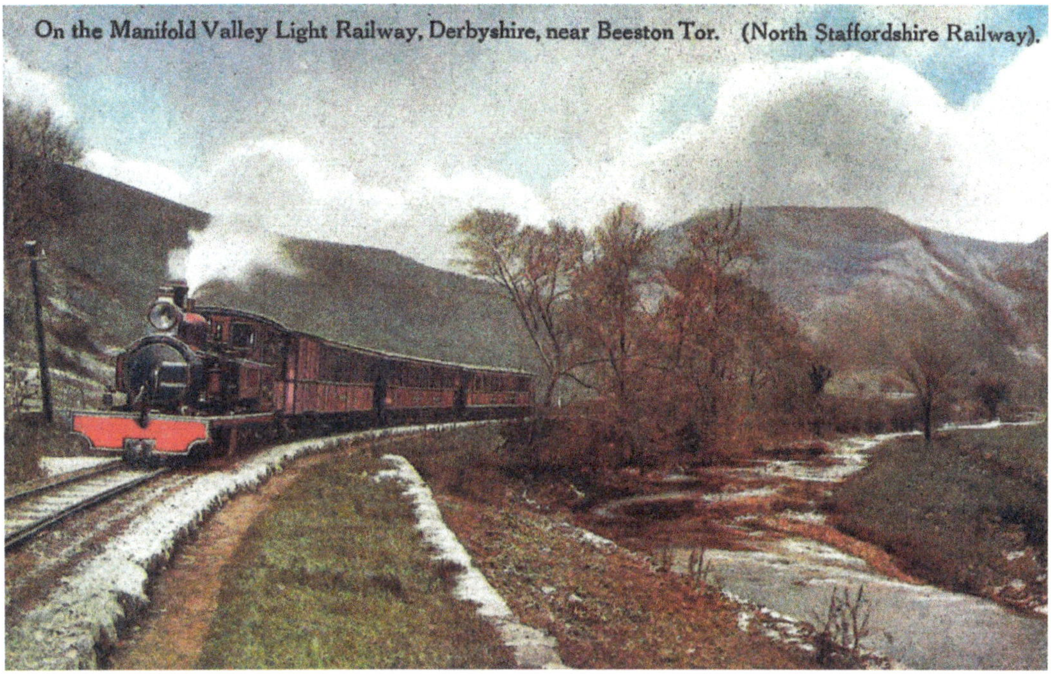

A colour postcard issued by the NSR to promote tourism to the scenic Manifold Valley. (Foxfield Railway Museum)

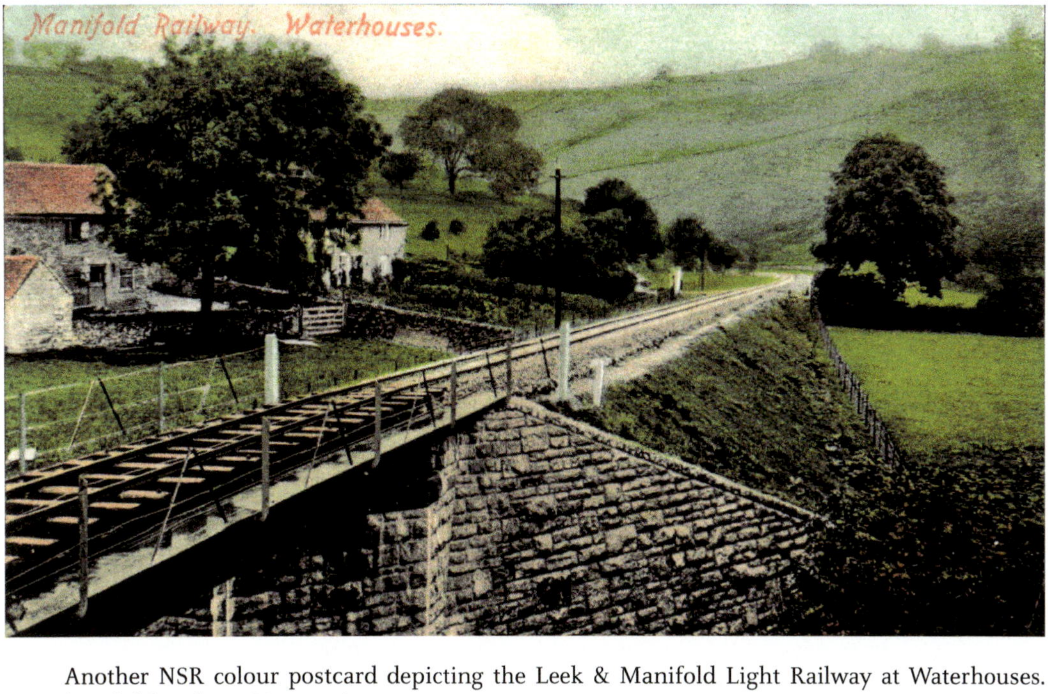

Another NSR colour postcard depicting the Leek & Manifold Light Railway at Waterhouses. (Foxfield Railway Museum)

The L&MVLR was first proposed in 1895 as a means of opening up the isolated villages around the Manifold Valley. Following the passage of the Light Railways Act in 1896, the Light Railway Commissioners granted a Light Railway Order for the Leek, Caldon Low & Hartington Light Railway of 6 March 1899. This was a 2-foot-6-inch-gauge railway running from Hartington to Waterhouses, with transhipment facilities at Hartington with the LNWR Buxton–Ashbourne line. The connection from Waterhouses to Leek was by a standard-gauge line, leaving the NSR Churnet Valley line at Leek Brook. The NSR agreed to work the line for a period of ninety-nine years at 55 per cent of the gross receipts. The engineer was Everard Calthrop, who was also responsible for the design of the locomotives and carriages that were inspired by his own Barsi Light Railway in India.

The Manifold line was opened between Waterhouses and Hulme End on 27 June 1904; the extension to Hartington not materialising. Sadly, the NSR line from Leek to Waterhouses was not ready and instead two NSR-owned steam omnibuses provided a connection. The Leek & Manifold quickly became popular for tourists in the summer months, and the NSR eagerly promoted, running through-trains from the Potteries, and in the pages of its official guide and colour postcards. Conversely, the local traffic was only small, with stations being inconveniently placed from the villages they were supposed to serve. Goods traffic, especially milk, was more profitable with milk trains running nightly from the Manifold Valley to Finsbury Park in London.

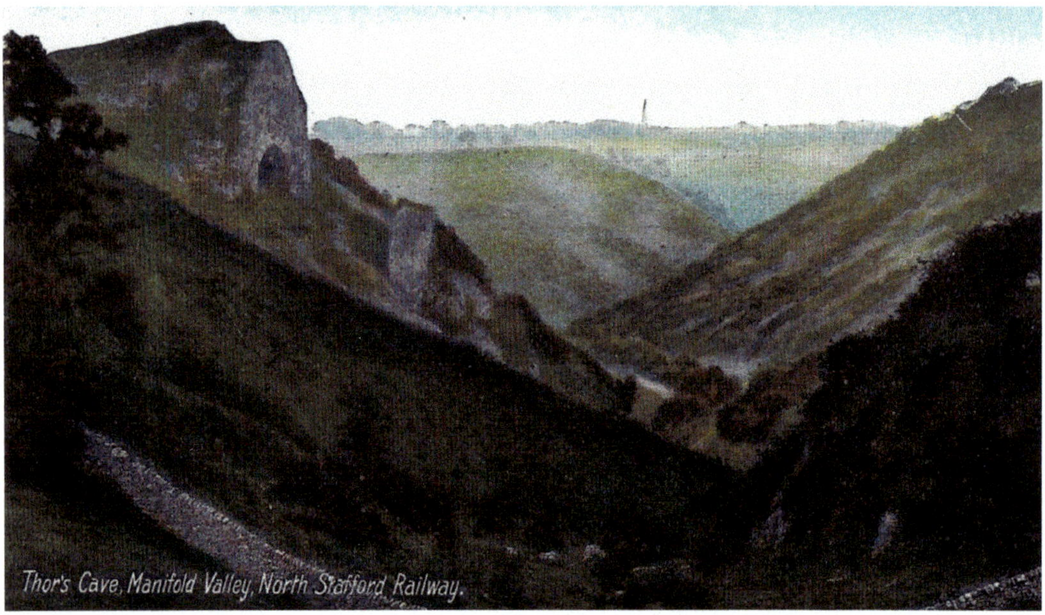

The NSR's publicity department was quick to promote tourism on the Leek & Manifold. This colour postcard was sent as a birthday card in March 1915 to Miss Jane Mills of Blythe Bridge. (Foxfield Railway Museum)

3

Edwardian Heyday

The NSR reached its highpoint in 1913. It was paying a 5 per cent dividend to its shareholders; income was at a record high and the track, locomotives and carriages were 'in excellent shape' with the latter being lit by electricity. According to the chairman the line had 'never been in such an excellent condition.' How it got there will be discussed below.

There was considerable investment in the permanent way, with a relaying programme beginning from 1904 which intended to relay 21 miles of track a year. In that year 7½ miles of the mainline was relaid with steel 90 lb 'bullhead' rails replacing

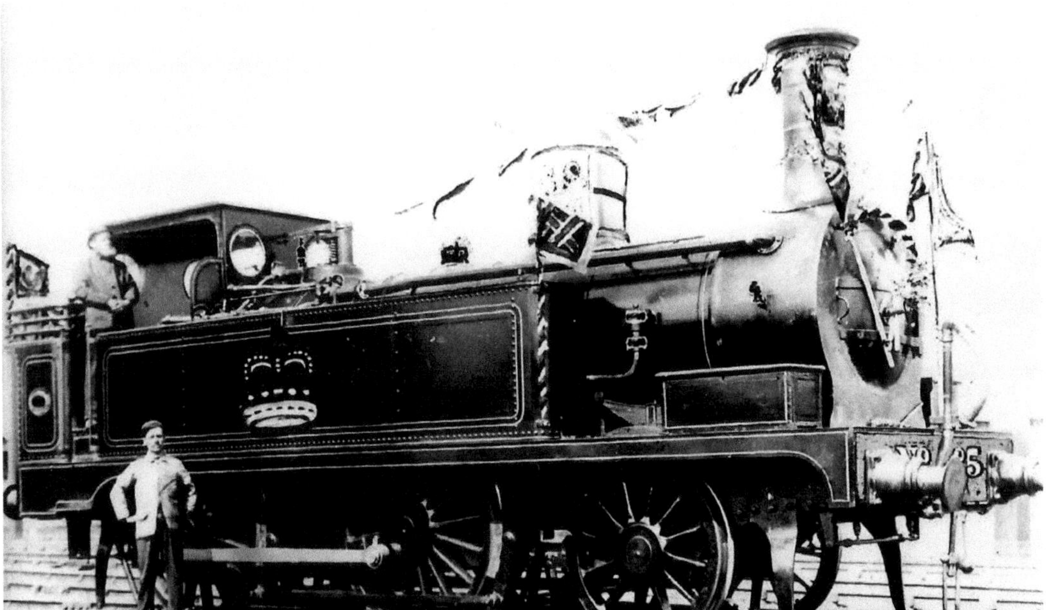

'B' Class No. 85 all dressed up in her finery to celebrate Queen Victoria's Diamond Jubilee, photographed at Stoke on 22 June 1897. (Foxfield Railway Museum)

the older 72 lb wrought iron rails. In 1905 it was forecast that seventeen miles per year would be replaced with steel rails. Ballast was limestone from the quarry at Caldon Low. This ambitious programme was somewhat frustrated during WW1: in 1915 only 13½ miles of track were relaid; 10 miles in 1916 and a mere 5 1/8 miles in 1918. Other modernisation to the track included the use of track circuits from 1916.

At the same time improvements were made to the rolling stock with the introduction of bogie coaches in 1906, and old grease axle boxes were replaced by oil. This set of five bogie coaches were destined for the summer Llandudno service and in winter for the Derby-Crewe workings. They had a high level of comfort and thanks to being semi-corridor, included lavatories for the first time. A second five-carriage set was built in 1907, and three identical lavatory composites, and further bogie coaches were built in 1908 which had full corridors but like the earlier bogie stock no corridor connections were provided. Despite this modernity, the NSR was still building six-wheelers as late as 1907 and close-coupled four-wheelers were still used on the Potteries Loop Line.

On the recommendation of the Board of Trade, a primitive communication cord was introduced in 1869 which rang a gong on the locomotive tender, and from 1883 the simple vacuum brake. The vacuum was created by operation of a valve on the locomotive; the vacuum actuated the brakes on each vehicle, and the degree of braking could be increased or decreased by the driver. The only problem with this system was that if the vacuum hoses had been incorrectly secured, or the train divided, the brakes would not work.

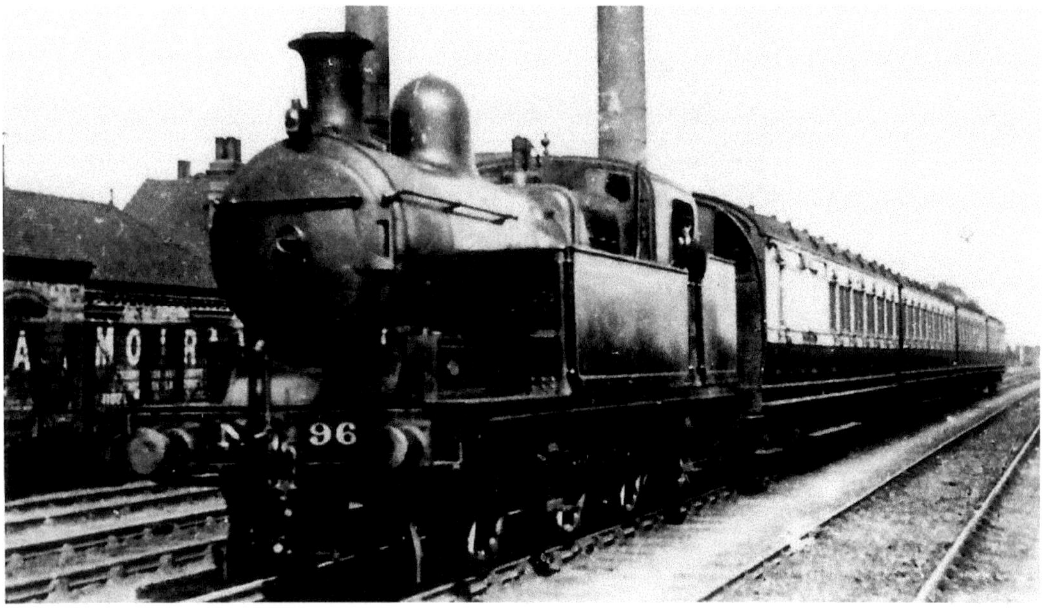

'New L' Class 0-6-2T No. 96 heads a train of NSR bogie stock approaching Tutbury with the Nestle factory in the background. (Foxfield Railway Museum)

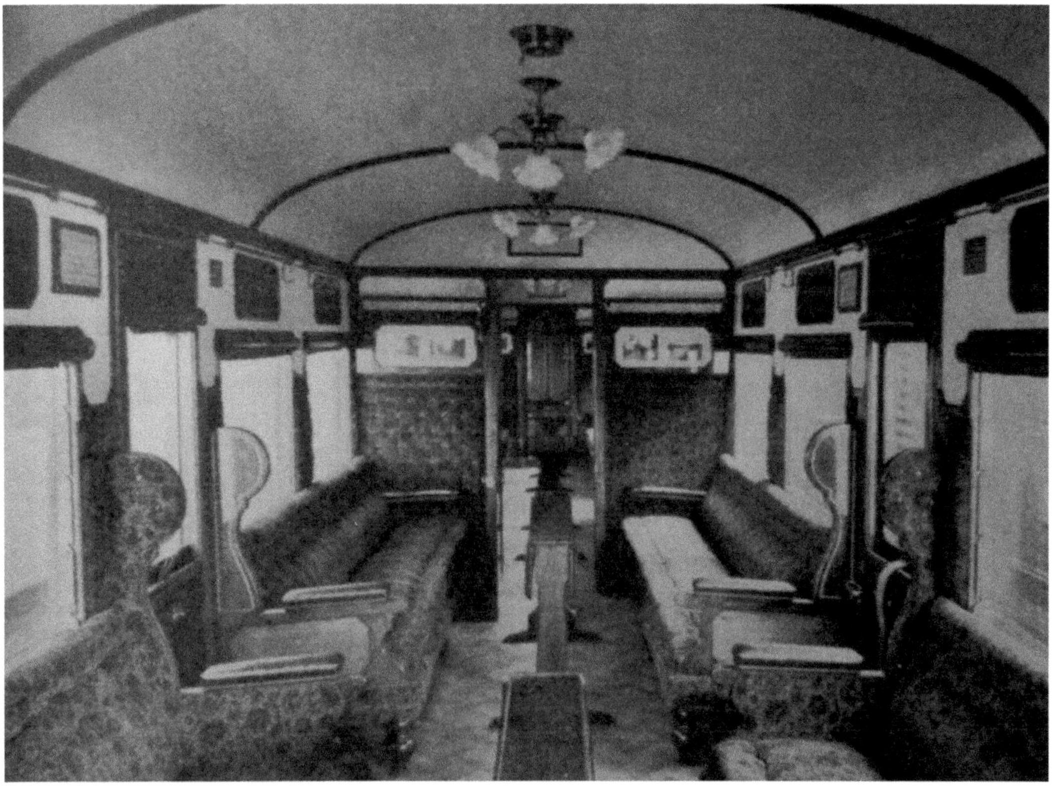

Interior of No. 290, one of two sumptuous first-class bogie saloons built at Stoke Works. The other was No. 143. (Foxfield Railway Museum)

Pretty much every carriage had been fitted with steam heat by 1919, with the exception of some of the older four-wheelers use on miner's trains.

Electricity

The Knotty is assured of a place in railway history as a pioneer of electric lighting: both on its stations and in its carriages, in the latter switching straight from oil to electric. In 1893, the same year that the Duke of Devonshire lit Chatsworth by electricity, the NSR approved the lighting of carriages as they were built at Stoke. The first carriage was so fitted in 1897, and conversion of existing stock began from the following year. New stock was fitted with electric lighting from 1899, and 115 were electrically lit by 1903, although some oil-lit coaches were still running as late as 1910.

At first the system was operated by a crated battery located in the Guard's compartment and an accumulator was installed at Stoke for recharging and supplying replacement batteries. A dynamo fitted to the carriage helped generate power, but

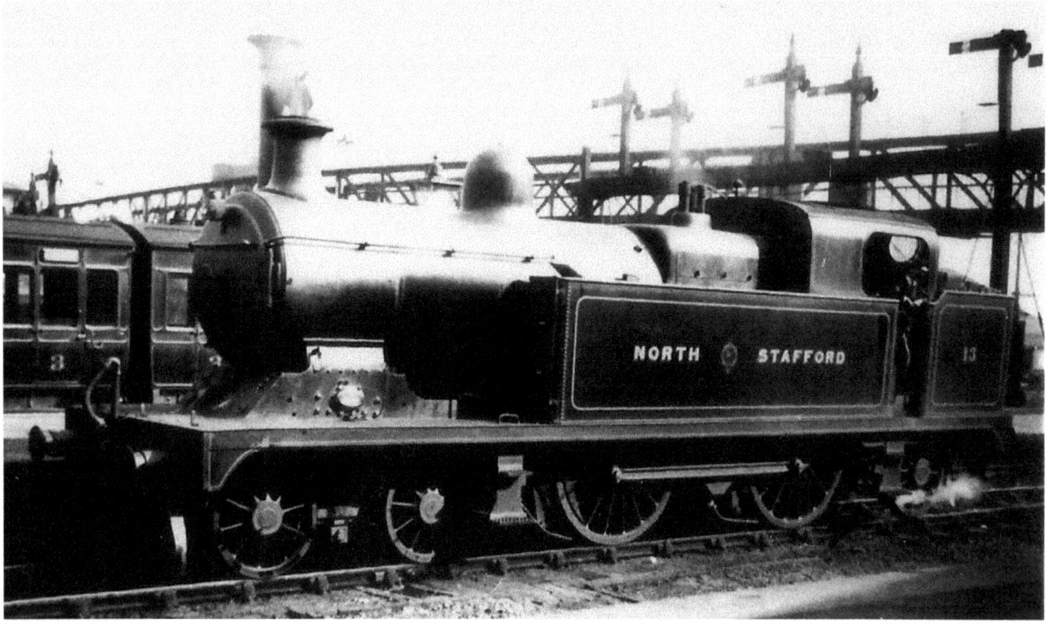

'K' Class 4-4-2T No. 13 was built at Stoke in 1912 and withdrawn by the LMS in 1935, who fitted it with Ross 'pop' safety valves and smaller 3-foot 3-inch bogie wheels, as the originals had tended to bind with the frames on sharp curves. (Foxfield Railway Museum)

this was often unequal to the task and the lights had a habit of going out when speed dropped below 10 mph. The bulbs used were quite dim, only equal to eight candle power: two bulbs were used to illuminate first-class compartments and only one for third. They were controlled by a switch in the guard's compartment. The cost of installing electric lighting was 'trifling' compared with oil, or even gas, and in the event of a collision was far safer.

NSR stations were also lit by electricity, the NSR having its own power station which also supplied the current for lighting all the signals in and around Stoke station. Electric tugs were also used to work the Harecastle canal tunnel from 1914.

Electricity wasn't just used to light carriages and stations but to provide motive power too. In 1917 three horses used at shunting the Oakamoor Copper Works sidings of Thomas Bolton & Sons were released by a battery-electric locomotive. Based on a similar design to one built for the Midland Railway in 1913. Built to a joint design of J.A. Hookham and the NSR electrical engineer A.F. Rock, the little machine weighed in at 17 tons, with the batteries located under two bonnets fore and aft. The locomotive operated at 250v and was capable of shifting loads of 90 tons at 10 mph on the level or 72 tons at 11 mph. When the Copper Works closed in 1963 it was withdrawn and placed in store before finding its way to the Museum of Staffordshire Life at Shugborough Hall, and later the National Railway Museum. During its working life

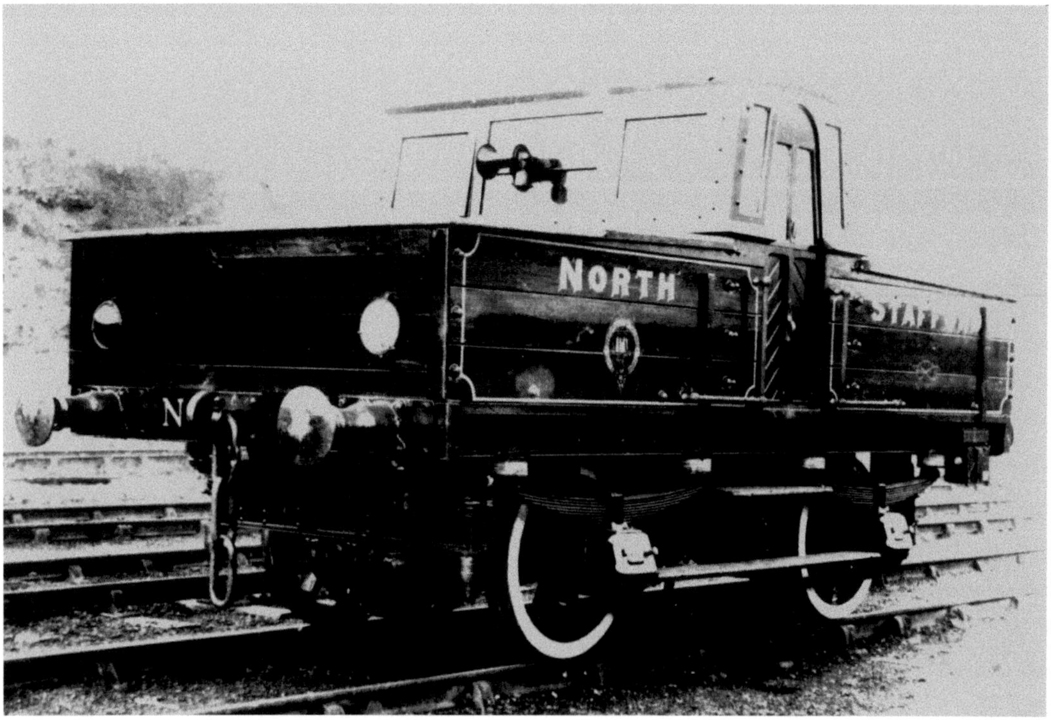

The unique NSR Battery Locomotive as built in 1917. Although only weighing 17 tons, it was capable of moving a load of 90 tons at 10 mph, and 72 tons at 11 mph. It is now part of the National Collection. (North Staffordshire Railway Study Group)

it only had two drivers: Arthur Adams, who joined the NSR in November 1916. After his untimely death in 1932, he was succeeded by Bill Prime, who first joined NSR as a Porter at Longton, drove the locomotive until 1963.

Improving the Image

The area served by the NSR is a juxtaposition of heavy industry and beautiful scenic moorland, and the NSR was quick to exploit the beauties of North Staffordshire. In 1890 it first published its *Official Holiday Guide*, which extolled the virtues of in particular the Churnet and Manifold Valleys. The NSR owned hotels at Stoke (the 'North Staffordshire') at Leek ('Churnet Hotel') and at Rudyard Lake ('Hotel Rudyard') where it also had an eighteen-hole golf course and provided other sporting amenities such as rowing and sailing on the lake. A delightful chalet-style station was built at Rudyard and the NSR published a series of colour postcards advertising the hotel, golf links and country walks. A series of official postcards of the Manifold Valley were also produced.

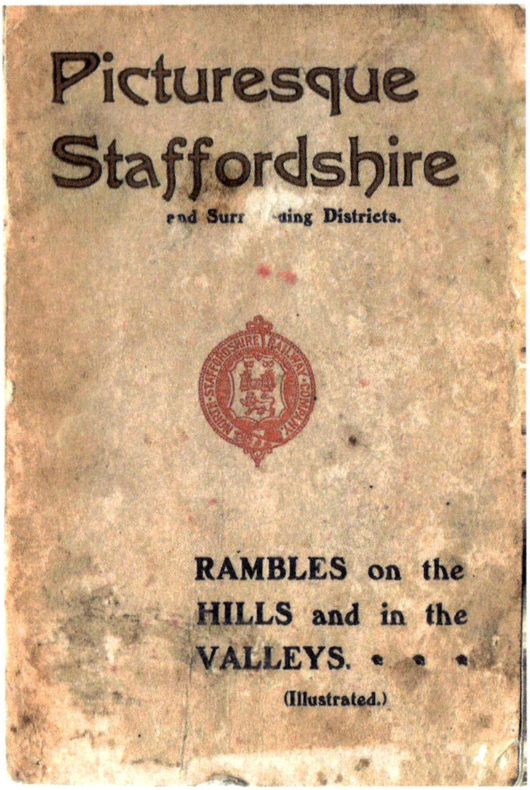

Left: The 'Knotty' had an excellent publicity department and published this illustrated guidebook to North Staffordshire from the 1890s. (Foxfield Railway Museum)

Below: The NSR issued series of colour postcards to promote tourism, and its own hotels including the Hotel Rudyard at Rudyard Lake. (Foxfield Railway Museum)

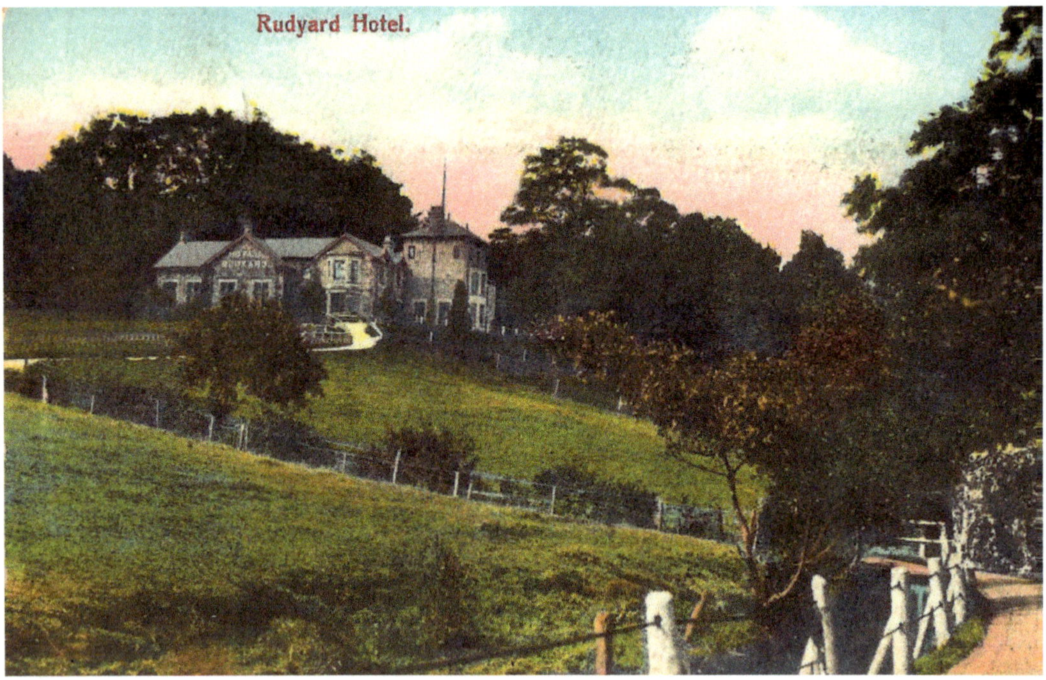

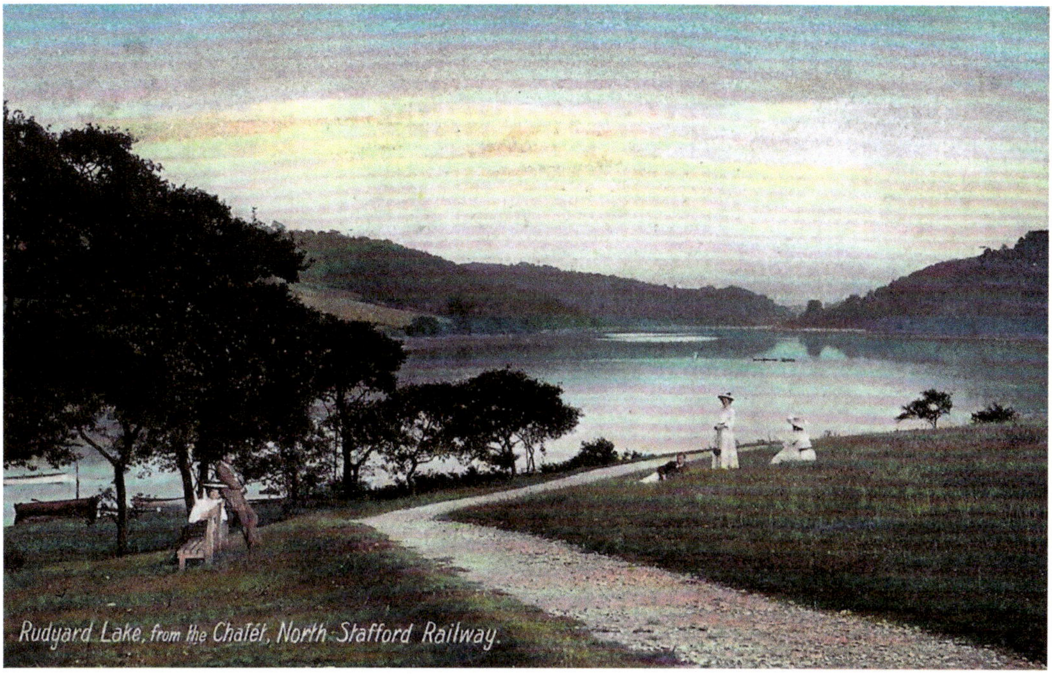

An Edwardian view of Rudyard Lake, published as a postcard by the NSR. (Foxfield Railway Museum)

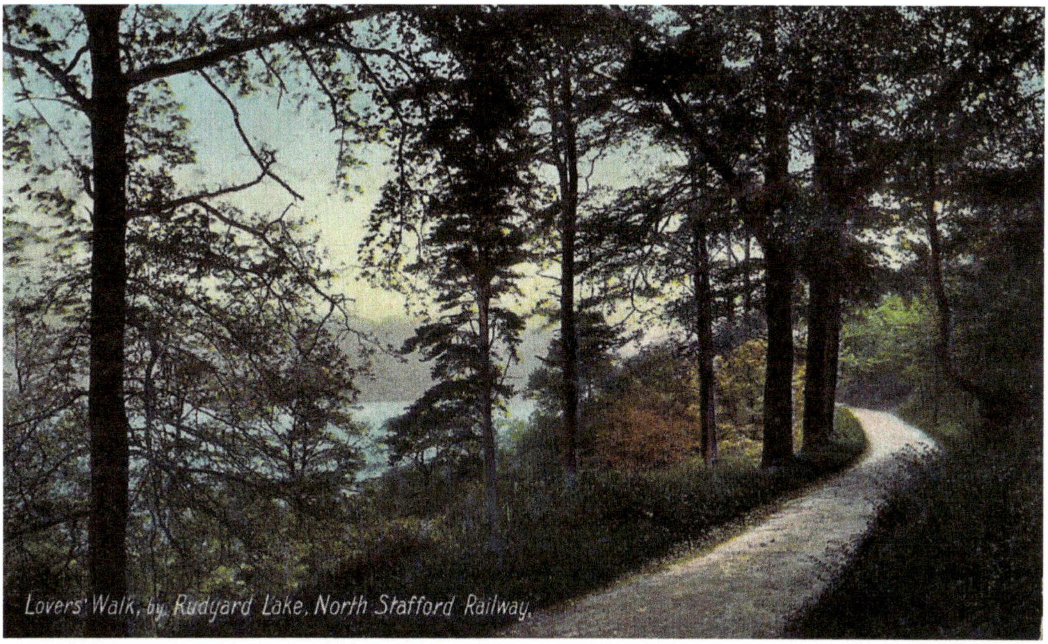

'Lovers Walk' by Rudyard Lake, depicted in an NSR colour postcard from the Edwardian era. (Foxfield Railway Museum)

Steam Railmotors

The NSR began experimenting with means of competing with the encroaching electric tramways. Trams had begun operating around the six towns in the 1880s as a steam tram service, and electric trams started running in 1899 thanks to the 'Potteries Electric Traction Co'. By 1905 the company had a system of 31 miles operated by 115 trams. For the Knotty, the fast, clean, electric trams severely dented its passenger figures, especially between Stoke and Newcastle: passenger numbers fell by 18,000 in 1901 to 600,000 across the entire network.

Something had to be done and the Chairman, Tonman Mosely, proposed in February 1905 the introduction of 'motor coaches on rails', to run through the most heavily populated parts of the NSR network. Three steam rail cars began running in June 1905 between either Silverdale or Trentham, but later extended to Leycett and on market days to Barlaston and Colwich. By 1908 they were maintaining a 15-minute service on the Potteries Loop Line.

These railmotors consisted of a small 0-2-2 tank locomotive built by Beyer, Peacock & Co. of Manchester permanently coupled to a 35-foot-long bogie saloon built by the Electric Railway & Tramway Carriage Co. of Preston. Accommodation was third class only, seating forty, with an additional small compartment for smokers and a tiny compartment for the guard and light luggage.

Up to the outbreak of the First World War they 'gradually extended their sphere of operation' but thereafter their use was curtailed. The heavy trainloads of wartime meant that they had to be replaced with conventional trains. The LMS, not really knowing what to do with them, withdrew them in 1923. Another innovation was the use by the Great Central Railway of a patrol-electric rail car between Macclesfield and Bollington from 1912 to 1934.

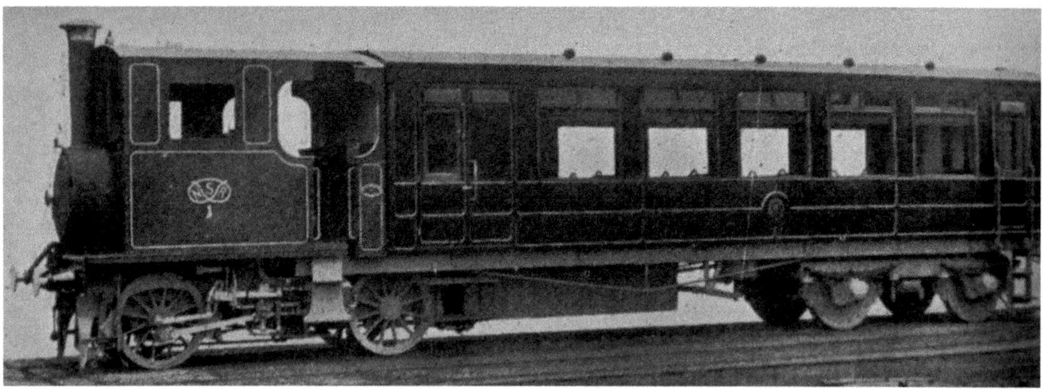

The NSR purchased three steam rail motors from Beyer, Peacock & Co. of Gorton to take the fight to electric street tramways, in which they were fairly successful. (Foxfield Railway Museum)

The other threat the NSR faced was road competition, from both steam buses and later more conventional diesel-engined vehicles. And indeed, it is likely that rather than the NSR's rail motor service curtailing further expansion of the tram system, it was the motor bus and motor car that did so. The response of the NSR's chairman in 1908 was to consider speeding up trains. He went on, however, to express the sentiment that 'first class passengers would soon tire of riding about in motors and return to the railway'. Sadly, such optimism was badly misplaced.

Expansion and Improvements

Despite this fierce competition, the NSR was able to take some comfort in the fact it was the 'Sixpenny Line' – sixpence being the average third-class fare – and with such low fares a loss of passenger numbers equated to only a small drop in revenue. In 1905, third-class bookings earned £90,284 out of a total passenger revenue of £110,170. Various suggestions were put forward to improving traffic, including a disastrous attempt in 1908 to run a passenger service 'entirely independent of the LNWR and MR'. Two years later the NSR attempted to abolish second class; lines like the Midland had done so in 1875. For several years the NSR had tried – and failed – to encourage second-class passengers to travel third class to avoid having to provide little-used second-class carriages. This innovation didn't work, as in such a class-conscious society letters were written to the local newspapers and to the board. Few as they were, second-class passengers complained about loss of status and that the third-class carriages were bare and draughty.

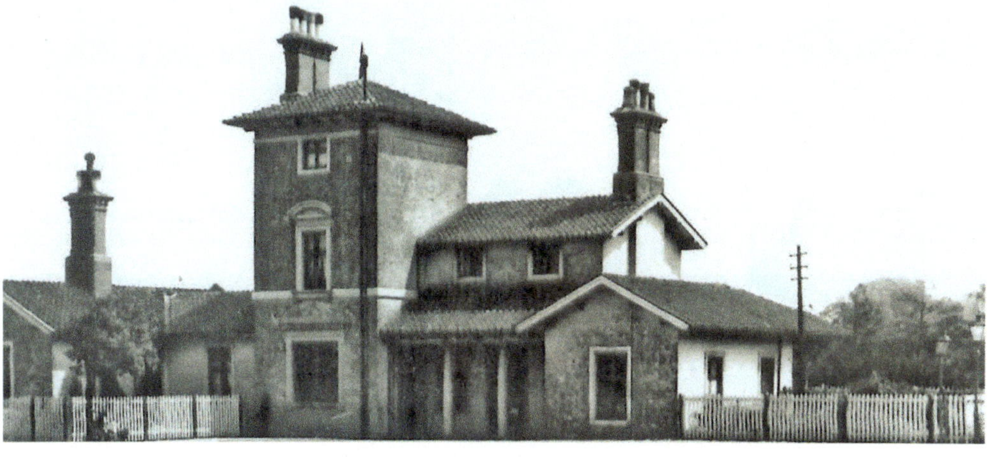

Trentham station was designed by Sir Charles Barry (architect of the Houses of Parliament) in an Italian villa style, making it stand out from the neo-Jacobean style of other NSR buildings. (Anthony Dawson)

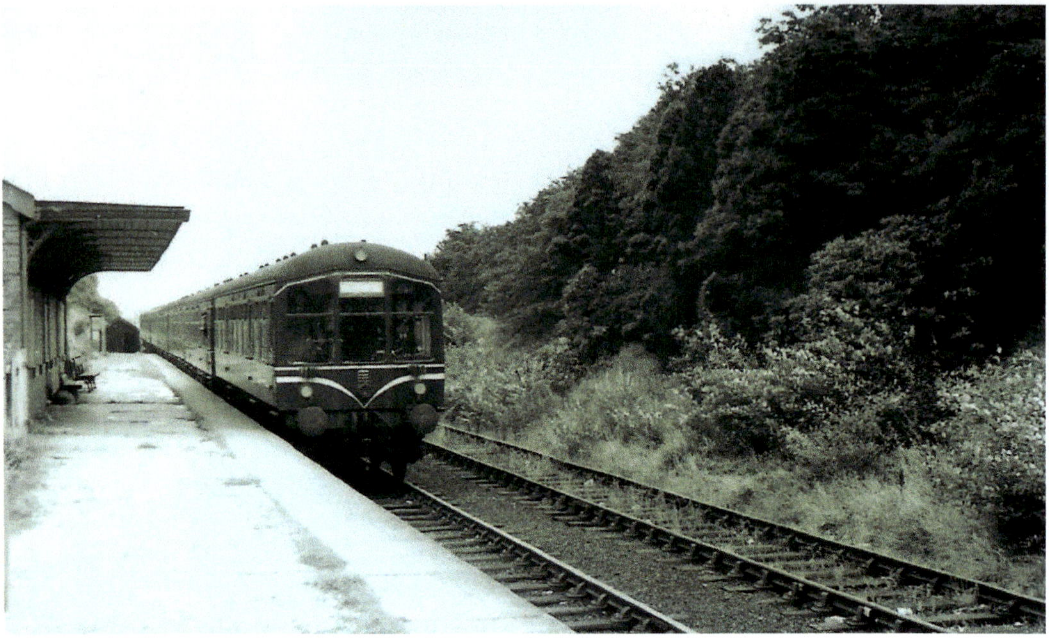

Trentham Park station mainly served day trippers looking for a fun day out at Trentham Park Gardens. Seen here in early DMU days. (Anthony Dawson)

The Knotty opened the last of its branches on 1 April 1910. The branch to Trentham Gardens had been authorised on 21 August 1907, under the same Act which also transferred to the Cheadle Railway (see pages 42 to 44) to NSR ownership. Trentham had grown into a large, respectable suburb and Trentham Hall and its 500-acre deer park and gardens proved a great attraction. By the time the branch was opened, however, road traffic was making major inroads into railway traffic and the only halt on the short branch – Hanford – closed in 1913. It was hoped that the Trentham Gardens branch would be extended to join the Pool Dam branch as the Trentham, Newcastle-under-Lyme & Silverdale Light Railway. It would have helped relieve a severe bottleneck in the Stoke area, but other than construction of a single bridge, work was shelved during the First World War and post-war traffic patterns, and ambitious plans for the Stoke area meant it was shelved indefinitely.

A Railway on Strike

All this progress was set against an atmosphere of unrest from the working men of the Knotty. Working hours of Victorian railwaymen were notoriously long, with engine drivers sometimes being on duty for twenty-four hours. The NSR made a reduction in working hours for drivers in February 1866 when their working week was cut to a mere seventy-two hours, which included an hour and a half on shed each. In November 1871, the NSR directors 'conceded the nine hours' system' to the men employed at Stoke Works in the locomotive and carriage and wagon departments. It was not applied to operational roles, however, where a working day of twelve hours was still the norm.

The long working days of operation staff was a major contributing factor for an accident at Stoke-on-Trent in the evening of 21 February 1872. The inspecting officer from the Board of Trade, Colonel Rich, recommended a reduction in the hours of signalmen from twelve hours to ten or eight hours as well as introduce shift work. He also felt that the accident had been caused due to the signalman on duty being too comfortable – and therefore inattentive – because they were provided with a high-backed seat. As a result, the NSR Board, instead of reducing working hours, decided to remove chairs, an example of which is on display at the Foxfield Railway.

The Regulation of Railways Act 1893 reduced the men's working hours nationally; it made 'excessive' hours illegal and introduced mandatory rest days. A further reduction of working hours took place in December 1896 when the foremen and yardmen at Stoke-on-Trent had their working day reduced to eight hours. The Truck Act (1896)

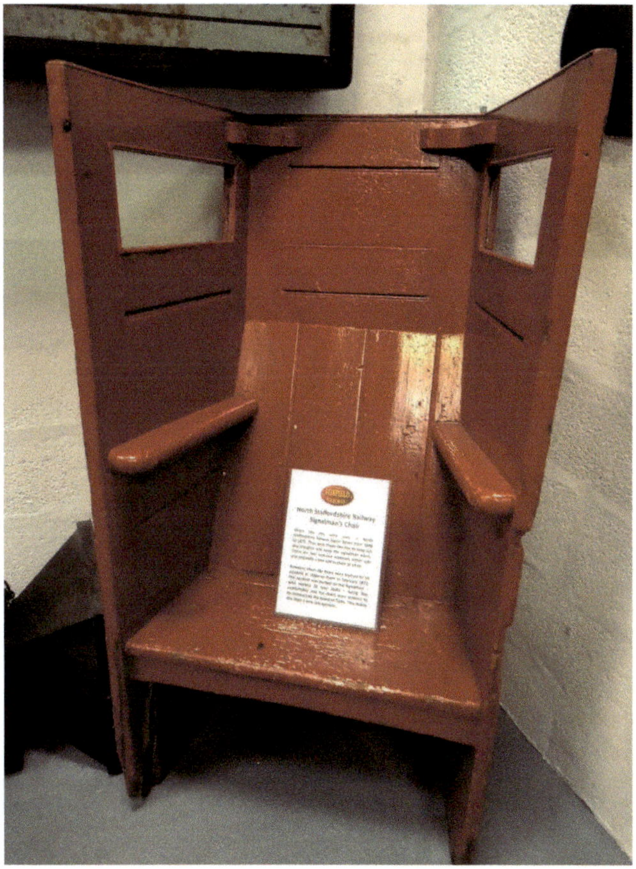

This NSR signalman's chair on display at the Foxfield Railway is a rare survivor – theoretically it should have been destroyed in 1872. (Anthony Dawson/Foxfield Railway Museum)

reversed some of the decisions of the 1893 Act, introducing fines from January 1897 – as much as 5*s* for even minor offences. Men who were late for work or spoke back to senior officers or passengers could be liable for a fine of up to 5*s* – about a third of a week's wages for a porter. A fine of 10*s* was levied if any 'negligence' delayed trains or damaged goods in transit; and £1 if there was any accident or incident that put a life in danger. Railwaymen nationally were unhappy with their low pay and long hours, with unrest during 1897 to 1898. The men of the NSR approached the board for higher pay, shorter days and better working conditions. The chairman remarked at the half-yearly meeting in February 1898 that such concessions by management would amount to £40,000 ('equal to a dividend of 1½ per cent'), but as the board was responsible to the shareholders he could not sanction such a move. He feared if the NSR were to increase its wages, then it would have a knock-on effect throughout the Potteries with a 'general rise in wages that would disturb and drive away a great deal of trade.' That said, however, various 'privileges' were granted in 1899 in working time, uniform, wages and promotion. The Railway Employment (Prevention of Accidents) Act of 1900 introduced further protections for railway workers.

There was further unrest in 1904 under the new chairman, Tonman Mosley, who instigated a period of strict economy and cost-cutting, which included cutting the working week of drivers and guards to five days with the considerable loss of income resulting. Wages, however, were increased two years later.

Staff of the NSR also had the support of the North Staffordshire Friendly Society, founded in 1887. By 1903 membership stood at 2,123 (out of a total workforce of around 4,000), which paid out in times of sickness, injury or death at work and also supported elderly and infirm railwaymen who were unfit for work. The NSR opened a savings bank in March 1908. A year later it had 3,448 members, and the board suggested that investors should be also able to purchase unissued stocks in the company without having to pay for an expensive broker. This meant employees were able to purchase NSR shares 'far below the actual value' and as result 'would watch very closely to see their interests were well protected'. Other concessions granted by the board were provision of coffins for those men killed in an accident at work, so long as they had been with the company for five years, and being able to keep uniform upon retirement.

In 1911, the NSR was involved in its first major strike. On 5 August around 1,000 members of staff of the Lancashire & Yorkshire Railway in Liverpool struck for an increase of wages and better working conditions. They were soon joined by railwaymen across the country. On the NSR it was reported that a guard was paid 22*s* per week, one of the lowest rates in the country, and would not receive the highest rates of pay – 32*s* 6*d* per week – 'until his 20th year in charge of a train'. Nationally, 100,000 railwaymen were earning less than £1 a week. The situation became so serious that the executive committees of the various railway trade unions joined forces to present their case to the government. The offer made by David Lloyd George, president of the Board of Trade, was not acceptable and there was a strike from 17 to 19 August 1911, bringing

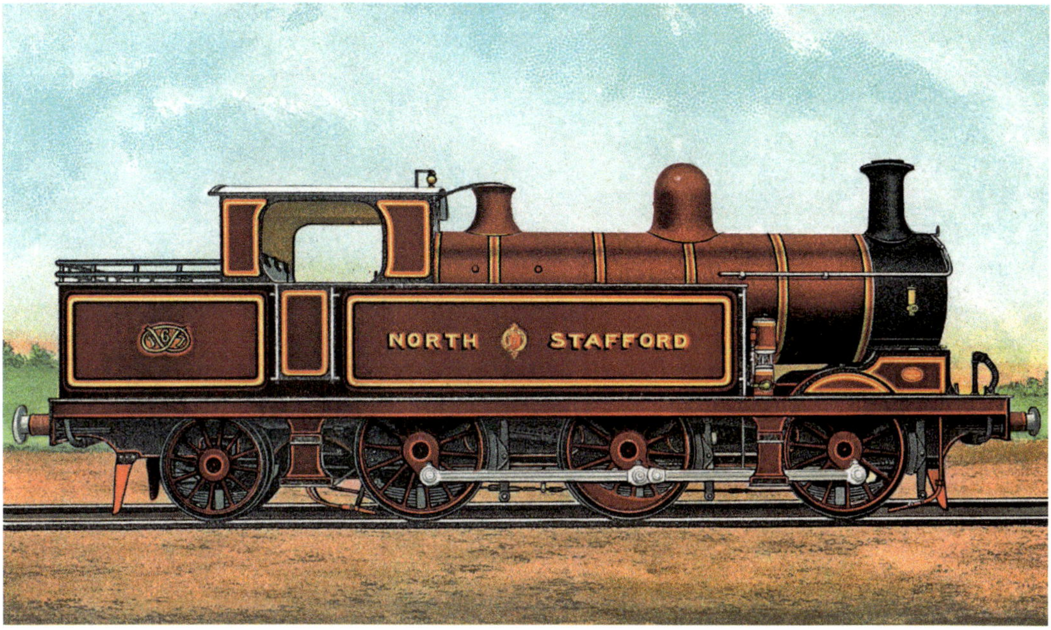

The 'L' Class was the first design introduced by John Adams as NSR locomotive superintendent. This contemporary colour print of 'L' Class No. 167, built by the Vulcan Foundry in 1903, shows the magnificence of the NSR livery. (Foxfield Railway Museum)

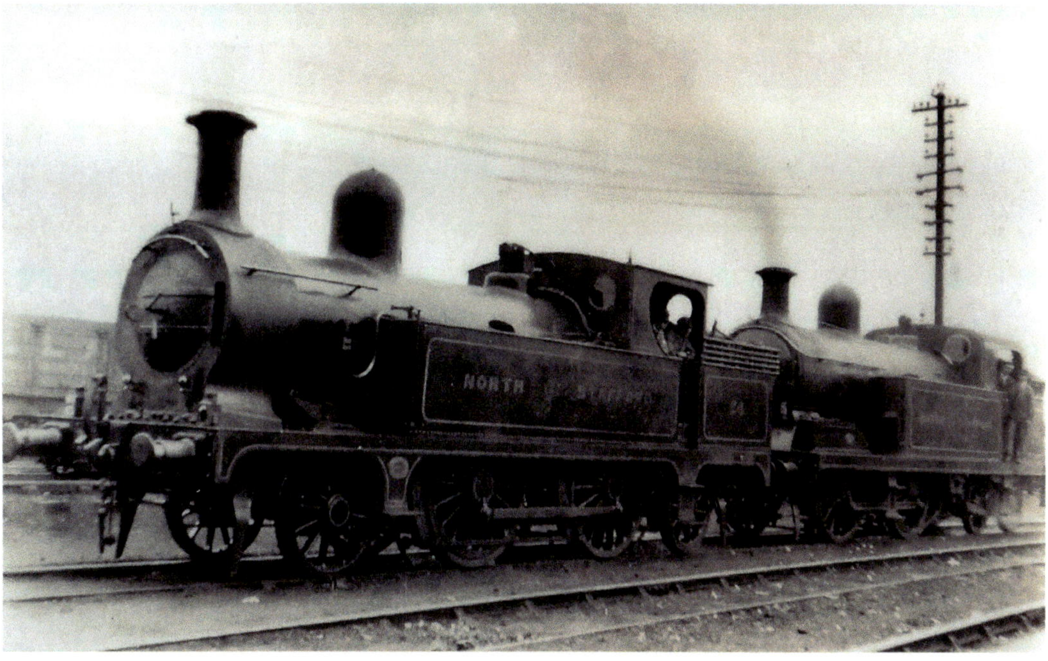

Rebuilt 'B' Class No. 24 (built 1886 as a 2-4-0T, rebuilt 2-4-2T in 1901) and its crew pose with an unidentified member of 'M' Class 0-4-4T, introduced in 1907. (Foxfield Railway Museum)

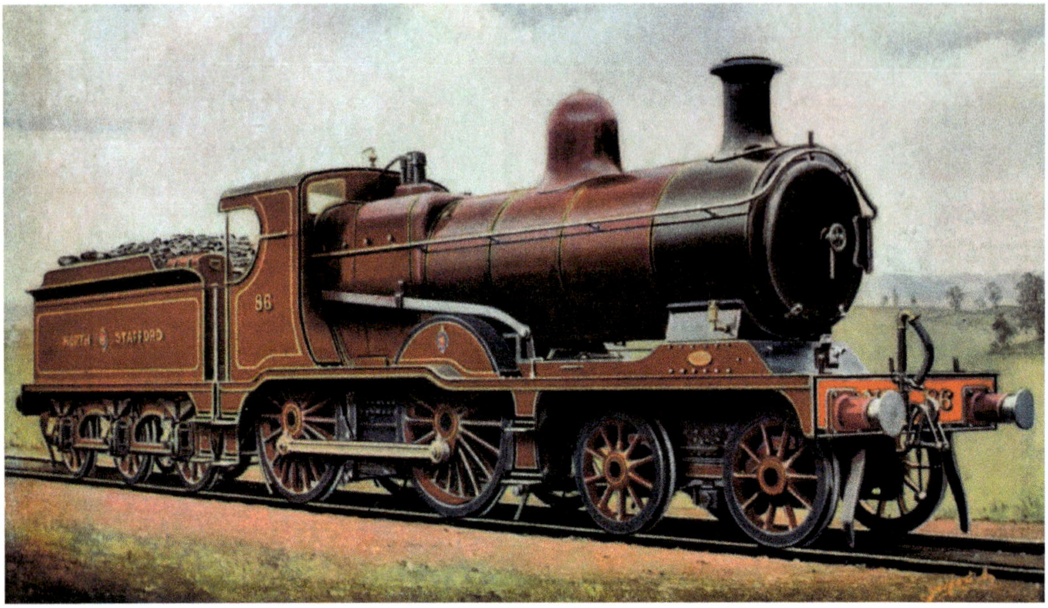

The NSR locomotive fleet was primarily tank engines, but four 4-4-0 'G' Class passenger locomotives were built in 1910 to handle heavy passenger traffic and through expresses from Crewe to Llandudno Junction. No. 86 was withdrawn in 1929. (Foxfield Railway Museum)

railway traffic almost to a standstill. In case of any unrest troops were sent north to Liverpool, Manchester and Birmingham, as well to guard key rail centres such as Crewe and the railways leading to Portsmouth and Southampton. In an attempt to break the strike, the LNWR offered double pay to any employee who turned up to work. On the NSR, there was a spate of stone throwing and window breaking by those on strike, with the windows of a number of signal boxes being broken where the signalmen had stuck to their post. Stones were also thrown at the few trains that were able to run.

Lasting only fifty hours, the 1911 strike saw an establishment of reformed 'Conciliation Boards' (formed in 1907) to listen to workers' grievances and to arbitrate between the trade unions and management. Furthermore, it was agreed for the 'immediate reinstatement of the strikers and lock-outs' as usually such men would be dismissed, never to be taken in the employ of the railway. Many of the grievances were met and a royal commission established. The *Staffordshire Newsletter* reported on 26 August 1911 that 'on Monday morning work was generally resumed', but the men of the Great Eastern and Midland refused to return to work. The men of the North Eastern also stayed out for several days longer, so did those of Liverpool Tramways, over the agreement to reinstate those who had been on strike, going so far as to threaten a national transport strike. Happily, those around the negotiation table saw sense.

4

War and Peace

War was declared between Britain and Germany at 11 a.m. on 4 August 1914. Everyone was looking forward to their summer holidays and predicted the war would be 'over by Christmas'. The news was greeted in Stoke-on-Trent 'peaceably' and with mixed emotions from the pulpits around the Potteries. Yet, in the following days several arrests were made of German and Austrian immigrants and their families who had been peaceably living in Stoke, Keel and Hanley, sometimes for generations, as being 'dangerous' to the war effort.[1] They were forbidden to travel more than 5 miles from their home; had to carry a permit at all times; were forbidden from owning a firearm, more than 3 gallons of any flammable substance and a homing or carrier pigeon; and those of age for military service (eighteen to thirty-five) were placed on parole.

Upon the declaration of war, the railways came under state control under the auspices of a Railway Executive Committee to ensure 'that the railways, locomotives, rolling stock, and staff shall be used as one complete unit in the best interests of the State for the movements of troops, stores and food supplies'.

The Railway Executive Committee was chaired by the president of the Board of Trade and consisted of the managers of the 'principal' railway companies, so it therefore did not include a representative of the NSR.

As far as the travelling public were concerned it was pretty much 'business as normal' who were looking forward to their summer excursions. Much to their disgust, the NSR cancelled all its long-distance excursions on and from 4 August to Liverpool, Blackpool and North Wales, which meant that there were scenes of great confusion and consternation at Stoke station:

1 The writer's family in Newcastle-upon-Tyne were among those considered 'illegal aliens' and his entire family was arrested, including his great-granny who was seven years old at the time.

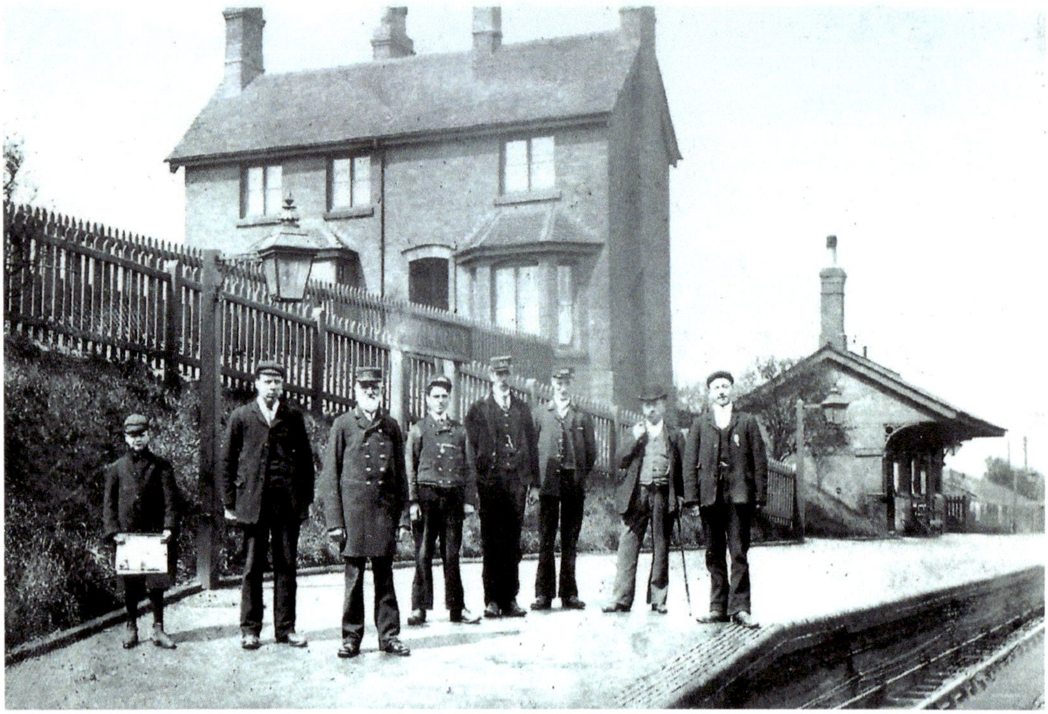

Stationmaster and staff at Normacot, *c.* 1890. The station opened in 1882 on the Crewe–Derby line. The first stationmaster was Mr Brookes on a salary of £60 p.a. plus the rent for his house. (Anthony Dawson)

> Hundreds of people who had built their hopes on going to the seaside on Monday were turned back, disappointed, only a few adopting the subterfuge of taking a two days' ticket with the hope of getting back after the troops had come through.
>
> (*Staffordshire Sentinel,* 4 August 1914)

The NSR, however, announced that despite 'circumstances over which the Railway Company has no control' leading to cancellation of many excursion trains for 'Wakes' (holidays) at the last moment it still managed to run those 'from the Potteries and Audley Line to Belle Vue, Manchester ... and the local excursions to the Manifold Valley, Leek, Rudyard, Rushton, Alton, Ashbourne, Trentham, Trentham Gardens etc... will run as advertised' (*Staffordshire Sentinel* 4 August 1914).

For their part, the LNWR immediately cancelled all excursions and the issue of excursion tickets 'and other tickets and reduced fares (except workman's tickets)' was cancelled forthwith. In order to give priority to troop trains many local trains were cancelled and there 'was a serious falling off in the ordinary local traffic' and rail traffic was generally disorganised over the entire NSR system. The local press thought the cancellation of so many holiday trains 'brought home a far more real appreciation of

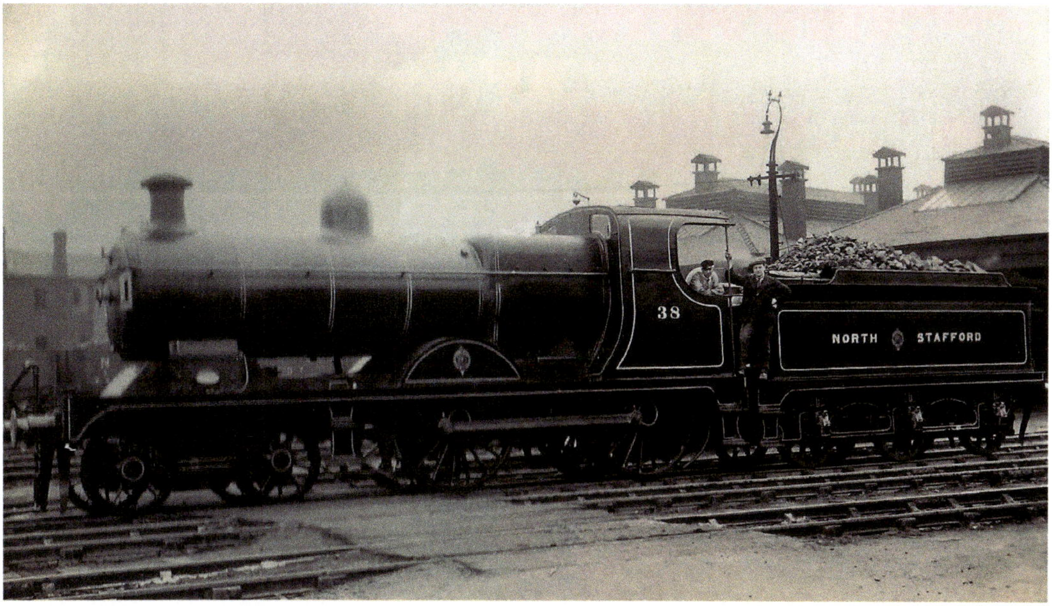

No. 38 was the sole member of 'KT' Class 4-4-0 passenger locomotive. Built at Stoke in 1912 as a tender version of Adams' 'K' Class 4-4-0T, her principal duty was to work summer expresses from Derby to Llandudno via Crewe. (Anthony Dawson)

the gravity of the situation'. The NSR did, however, resume booking of long-distance excursions on Friday 21 August and were to run until the end of the month, but there would be no excursions at Christmas.

During 1915 the Railway Executive Committee ordered a 'drastic reduction' in train mileage in order to 'minimise the consumption of coal and favour other coal consumers'. As a result, from February the 4 p.m. from Euston to Stoke and thence Manchester was cancelled. Day and half-day excursion tickets were to be discontinued, along with 'pleasure party tickets' for football matches and going to the races. Excursions to Liverpool, Manchester and Birmingham were also cancelled, along with all Easter and Whitsun specials other than weekend tickets. Unsurprisingly, there was a flurry of complaints to the local press. From January 1917 some 20 per cent of all passenger trains were stopped at the government's request to give priority to troop and munitions trains. While in May, W.D. Phillipps announced that 'if the war continued through the next winter the service would be further reduced' and that the board were contemplating 'the advisability of closing certain branches altogether'. Despite this, the excursions during Wakes Week 1917 were absolutely packed and it was necessary to 'put on four or five relief trains to Blackpool, and a similar number to North Wales'. Relief trains were also run to local beauty spots, including Rudyard Lake and Trentham Gardens.

By the summer of 1918 some excursions were running 'as adequately as the Government restrictions will allow'. 'More people,' reported the *Staffordshire Sentinel,*

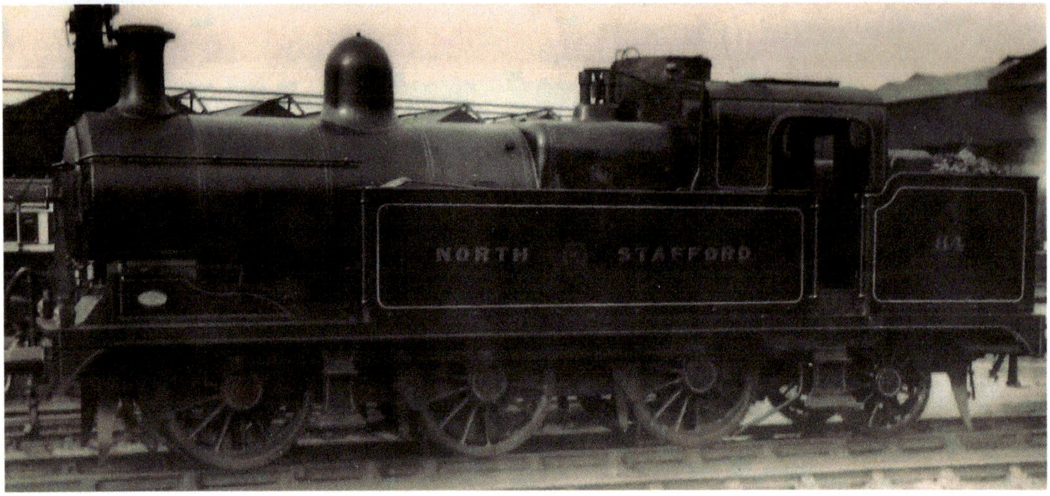

'New L' Class No. 64, one of the second batch built in Stoke in 1913, which carried a Belpaire firebox from new. The eight locomotives in this batch were also fitted with hot-water injectors and condensing gear. (Foxfield Railway Museum)

'are going away than in any other war year.' This was partly as a result of the LNWR stopping bookings for its excursions. As many as fifteen trains to Blackpool and seven for North Wales left Stoke on 3 August 1918:

> Every train was full, and every train was of extraordinary length, some having to draw up, even at the long platform at Stoke after the front and centre carriages had been filled. Besides, there were the usual trains to Crewe, carrying extra coaches and all occupied to the utmost extent. Mr E.D. Grassett, OBE, the outdoor traffic superintendent, was on duty on the platform and personally supervised the traffic, adding extra carriages where necessary.
>
> (*Staffordshire Sentinel*, 3 August 1918)

Despite the apparent success of the summer excursions, the Railway Executive Committee cancelled all Christmas excursion trains and instead existing services were to be augmented.

Gone to War

By February 1915 some 504 staff were serving in the armed forces. As in the Boer War, the NSR directors showed generosity to its fighting men and their families at home. They guaranteed a job upon their return and provision for their wives, families and dependents totaling £2,500 per year. In January 1916, 701 men had enlisted, of whom twenty-three had lost their lives. A year later, in 1917, 859 men had joined up; forty-seven had been sadly killed and fifty wounded. In order to replace their men, some 147 women had been taken on as clerks, ticket collectors, porters and even guards, a significant increase on the seventy-one employed pre-war. The number of women employed would eventually rise to a total of 216.

This wasn't the first time that NSR personnel had gone to war: many volunteered to serve in the Second Boer War (1899–1902), including John Henry Adams, the future locomotive and carriage superintendent. In 1899, he became the assistant manager of the SECR Works at Ashford in Kent, but didn't remain in post very long as he volunteered to serve with the Derbyshire Imperial Yeomanry. Enlisting as a trooper, he returned home in 1902 as a quartermaster sergeant and took up his appointment at Stoke as locomotive superintendent in March 1902. Twenty-one members of the NSR St John Ambulance Brigade volunteered to serve in South Africa during the Boer War tending the wounded. Other NSR men such as shunter George Steventon from Hanley was recalled to serve in his old unit, the Army Service Corps. His brother was also a railway employee and reservist.

On the home front the NSR formed its own Volunteer Training Corps commanded by J.A. Hookham in November 1914 and made up of able-bodied men aged over seventeen forming a part of the larger North Staffordshire Volunteer Training Corps. Hookham was already involved in the NSR Rifle Club. Their initial uniform was a red arm band 'with the letters "GR" inscribed thereon'. Because so many men of service age had volunteered into the forces – despite the railways being a protected occupation – the VTC had several rather derogatory nicknames based on their GR arm band and age of the members – George's Wrecks, Grandpa's Regiment and Genuine Relics. Grey-green rather than khaki uniforms were authorised in 1915. The training consisted of rifle drill, foot drill, and rifle shooting. The NSR Rifle Club had been in existence for some years. It had its own range at Winton Square and a .303 range at Pratt's sidings in Fenton. The VTC had to use borrowed or privately purchased weapons that were 'non-service', i.e. obsolete. The NSRVTC was formed 'to protect vulnerable parts of the system' in case of enemy action. The war also saw an expansion of the NSR St John Ambulance Teams, increasing from five brigades to seven, totaling 300 fully trained men by 1917.

During the course of the war around 100 men from the NSR were allowed to volunteer to go to France to work on railway construction near Abbeville. Drawn primarily from the Engineers' Department, they were superintended by G.J.R. Gossling and V.E. Vickers.

One of the major losses to the company early in the war was the death of J.H. Adams, the locomotive superintendent who had done so much to modernise and standardise the NSR locomotive fleet on 7 November. He was succeeded by John Albert Hookham. In 1917, the indefatigable manager W.D. Phillipps was elected to the board. Phillipps had come to the NSR in 1882 after having held managerial positions on the LNWR. He retired in 1919 after thirty-seven years in railway service, having 'gradually built up the reputation of the [NSR] Company' to a 'flourishing position'.

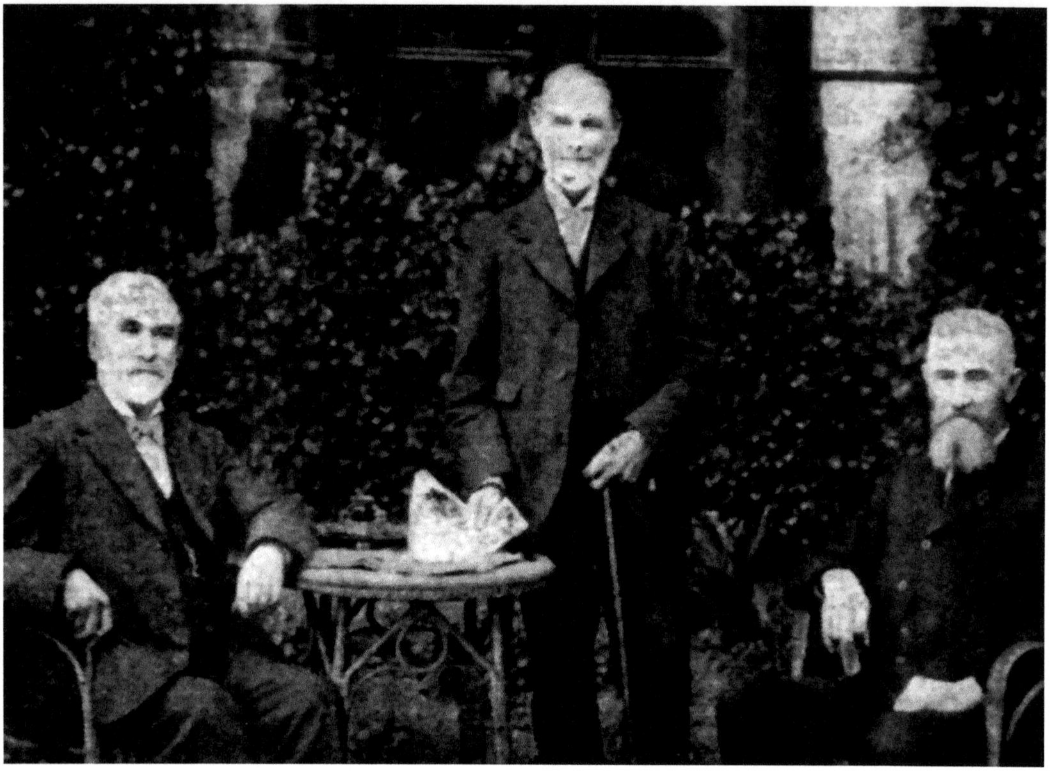

NSR Octogenarians: W. D. Phillipps photographed in June 1919 at the time of his retirement, together with Mr J. Rice (left) the assistant general manager who joined the NSR in 1876, and Mr M. Curbishley (right), the mechanical signal inspector 1886–1917. All three turned eighty in 1919. (Anthony Dawson)

Troops and Stretchers

During the first six months of the war the NSR carried some 70,000 servicemen, 2,860 horses and wounded men heading in the opposite direction. Twenty-one ambulance trains were handled in Stoke during the course of 1916, each carrying around 200 men. Between November 1916 and the middle of February 1917, sixty ambulance trains ran via Stoke to Manchester or Yorkshire, and during the whole of that year Stoke dealt with twenty-five such trains, carrying 3,215 wounded men. The *Staffordshire Sentinel* described one such arrival:

> 120 wounded soldiers arrived at Stoke at 6.5pm on Sunday evening from French hospitals by a special Lancashire & Yorkshire train; no fewer than a hundred required stretchers, but so smartly did the ambulance workers carry out their duties, that every patient had been removed by 7.25 pm to the North Staffordshire Infirmary.
>
> (*Staffordshire Sentinel*, 6 March 1916)

Providing invaluable help were the Volunteer Motor Corps, a similar organisation to the VTC (see page 67) but formed from those who owned their own motor car or similar motor vehicle. It had been formed in April 1915 and by January 1916 consisted of sixty-six drivers and orderlies, thirty-five motor cars, two motor lorries, three motorcycles, and two motor ambulances. There were also twelve 'ambulance trailers', which carried stretchers. These 'ambulance trailers' were supplemented by those loaned by Chatterly Whitfield Colliery and Robert Heath & Sons. On one occasion the VMC were able to clear 121 wounded men in 60 minutes from Stoke station to hospital. They were:

> In charge of Mr Will H. Brain [and] worked splendidly, and as there was no shortage of cars and trailers, the periods of waiting were very short. At the station, the Hanley, Birchenwood, and North Staffordshire Railway Divisions of the St John Ambulance Brigade, and the Newcastle and Hanley Red Cross Detachment, worked under the direction of Acting Corps Superintendent Hey, and the way in which the wounded were handled was praiseworthy.
>
> (*Staffordshire Sentinel*, 6 March 1916)

Later in the year the *Sentinel* reported with pride how a train of 116 wounded men – ninety-nine stretcher cases, seventeen sitting – were disembarked and dispatched to Stoke War Hospital in only 22 minutes. Food and drink, together with free cigarettes, were liberally doled out to the men, the latter donated by Barlow & Sons of Longton.

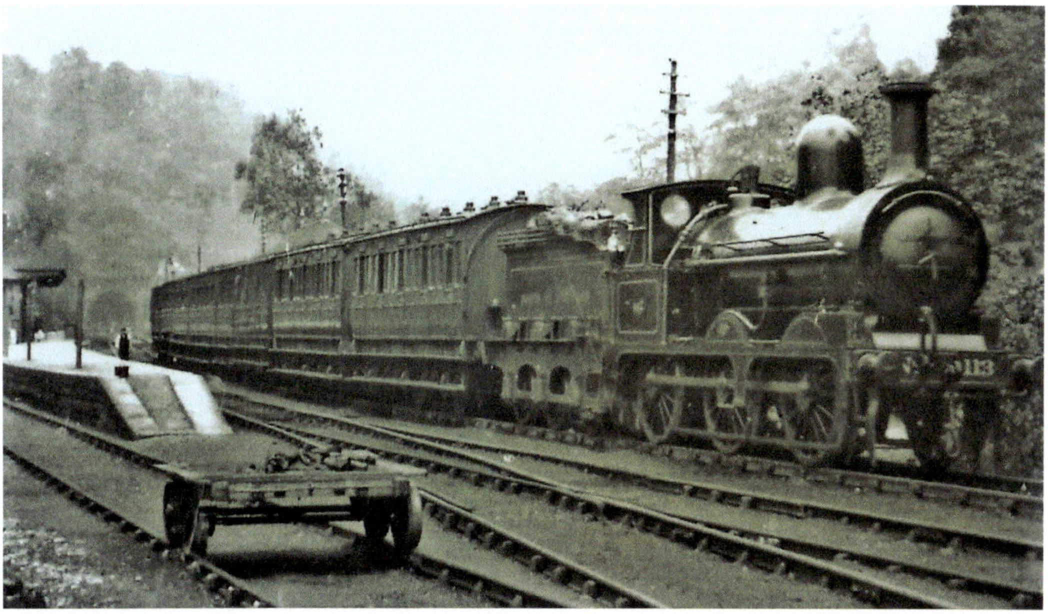

A passenger train rattles through Oakemoor on the Churnet Valley Line, headed by No. 113, a 0-6-0 goods tender engine built by the Vulcan Foundry in 1872. It was rebuilt twice – in 1896 and 1909 – before being withdrawn in December 1928. (Anthony Dawson)

1918: Internal Battles

Seventy years after the NSR faced its own internal struggle for survival and despite war raging in Europe, from 1917 to 1918 the NSR faced its own battle. During 1917 there had been a 'sudden volume of agitation ... against everything the company did'. The *Staffordshire Sentinel* reported in August 1917 that the NSR was 'in Crisis', the charges against the company being poor service and poor connections with trains of other companies especially the LNWR; high fares and especially high goods rates. In another echo of seventy years before, there were arguments for the NSR to amalgamate with the LNWR.

A committee was organised by the Board of Trade to examine the goods rates in North Staffordshire, to which the NSR was not invited. This committee recommend amalgamation of the NSR with another larger concern in order to lower goods and passenger rates, economy of working, and higher levels of customer service. This was 'welcomed' by 'Commercial and Industrial Circles in North Staffordshire'. Furthermore the:

> Recent recommendation of the Board of Trade Committee dealing with iron and coal trades after the war that a local Court of Inquiry should be appointed to inquire into the circumstances of the North Staffordshire Railway, and to recommend immediate action... the North Staffordshire's high rates, it is contended, are a check to industrial expansion.
>
> (*Derbyshire Advertiser and Journal*, 29 June 1918)

Even though the war was not over, a full inquiry was heard, presided over by Mr Rowland Whitehead KC in Stoke Town Hall from 23 to 25 October 1918. The NSR was represented by Mr Honoratus Lloyd, who noted he had 'difficulty in ascertaining under what sanction the Inquiry was held'. He also complained that the NSR had 'not been invited to give evidence before the committee' and that the 'first thing they knew about it was the Report and the Board of Trade refused a copy of the evidence.' The NSR then decided to withdraw from the proceedings as 'the Inquiry [w]as not legally authorized' (*Staffordshire Sentinel*, 23 October 1918).

Arrayed against the NSR were the mayor and Stoke-on-Trent Corporation and trade organisations including the North Staffordshire Colliery Owners' Association, the Blast Furnace Owners' Association, the North Staffordshire Labour & Trades Council, the North Staffordshire Chamber of Commerce, and the Staffordshire Potteries China Manufacturers' Association. Also included were various district councils. They were essentially representatives of all the major industries in North Staffordshire.

Representing the BoT, Mr Thorne Drury described how the high goods rates of the NSR 'penalised' the industry of the region to the tune of £50,000 per year, especially the pottery and silk trade. Mr W. Simons, managing director of the Shelton Iron,

Steel, & Coal Company, while he had no argument with the staff of the NSR, noted their goods charges were too high, costing him £55,000 to £60,000 per year in 'excessive' fees. Mr Wheatley, a brick and tile manufacturer, estimated NSR goods charged were '50 per cent in excess'. He also complained about the lack of a local presence on the NSR Board with no local manufacturers being included other than Major Wedgwood. Robert Shenton of Messrs Wedgwood & Co. similarly agreed that the NSR's rates were 'very much higher' than those of other companies, and that there was a very high rate of breakages of his pottery, which made the high goods rates even more inexcusable. Further discussion took place as to the poor provision at most stations for goods traffic, poor provision of goods shed and warehouse space. Other complaints levied against the NSR included the old-fashioned, 'quaint' way of dealing with excursion tickets; that season tickets were too expensive and passengers in general 'dealt very harshly with'. Passengers on the NSR were paying 2.50*d* per mile while those on the GWR 0.6*d* per mile. Connections with other lines, particularly the LNWR and Midland, were very poor. Whitehead's report was published on 6 December 1918 and proposed that the NSR be nationalised or be amalgamated with a larger concern, preferably the LNWR as it already had running powers over a large part of the NSR system. The report found that it represented 'a fair indication of local opinion' and that even if the NSR charges were not too high the 'impression current in the district [was] an important fact'. The inquiry did conclude, however, that the NSR's goods charges were 'exceptionally high' with the knock-on negative effect to local business and members of the public (*Staffordshire Sentinel*, 30 January 1919).

Unsurprisingly, the NSR published its own reply, which was printed in the local newspapers. The NSR contented its maximum goods rates were much below the maximum it could legally charge, and that the LNWR had powers to charge higher rates for mineral traffics than it could. The rates for pottery were high because it was fragile, bulky, and not economic to ship by rail. Finally, the company further noted that since 1914 every industry in Britain had increased charges by 75 per cent – all except the railways.

This reply did little to mollify the industrialists or travelling public of the Potteries. A public meeting was held in Stoke on 1 January 1919, chaired by the mayor, Alderman W. E. Watson. The meeting greeted the BoT Inquiry and ensuing report by Rowland Whitehead KC 'with satisfaction' that 'the whole of the allegations made by the Corporation ... were declared by the Commissioner to be fully established'. The corporation therefore resolved:

A) That the strongest possible representations be made to the President of the Board of Trade with a view to his immediately taking such actions as will provide the district of North Staffordshire with equal facilities – for both goods and passengers – as are enjoyed by other industrial centres.

B) That a deputation consisting of the Mayor [and alderman and councilors] be appointed to attend upon Sir William Marwood of the Railway Department of the Board of Trade, to make such representations.

(*Staffordshire Sentinel*, 30 January 1919)

In support of the NSR were Kerr, Stuart of Stoke-on-Trent, then the largest engineering works in the Potteries ('probably larger than the next six engineering firms combined'), who had not been asked for their opinion at the inquiry. They would not have become involved in the dispute had it not been for the 'injustice' that they perceived done to the NSR, especially by 'the Town Clerk and his Cabal'. Kerr, Stuart had worked with the NSR for twenty-four years, had an excellent working relationship and had always been granted the best facilities available (*Staffordshire Sentinel*, 13 February 1919).

Unfortunately, the NSR's 'reply' cast aspersions regarding the 'dignity and honesty of the council' – especially the comment by Kerr, Stuart & Co. regarding the town clerk – was met with a dignified response. At a meeting of the borough council on 27 February the mayor issued his own reply to that of the NSR and Kerr, Stuart describing the latter's comments as contemptible.

Not only did the mayor and corporation consider the NSR's memorandum 'contain[ed] numerous mis-statements' but it was 'evasive'; if it had been subject to cross-examination 'it could be torn to ribbons'. The corporation felt the NSR's assertion that the Court of Inquiry was illegal besmirched the mayor and corporation as it was they who had proposed the inquiry. Furthermore, it was felt that the NSR's reason for its withdrawal from the proceedings 'not sufficient'. It also transpired that the NSR had, in order to garner their support at the inquiry, met with the goods managers of those railways that connected with or ran over the NSR but they declined to do so. The NSR may also have overshot their mark in questioning the neutrality of Mr Whitehead KC, who led the inquiry, claiming he was predisposed 'in favour of the traders' and that 'instead of a judicial document, it reads as though he held a brief from the traders'. In closing his own response to the NSR the mayor stated: 'It only led them to this opinion: that this Company had no reply to make to the traders and to the community.' (*Staffordshire Sentinel*, 28 February 1919)

Rumours abounded in March that the NSR was about to be amalgamated with the LNWR or that 'the Board of Trade was arranging with the North-Western and Midland Companies' to jointly work the NSR for a period of two years. During the same month, the North Staffordshire Trader's Association sent a successful deputation to the NSR regarding claims for loss of goods destroyed or damaged in transit. The inquiry was even discussed in Parliament by the MP for Hanley, but no timetable was set for its recommendations to be acted upon. This was probably because this was at a time when the future of the railways was being discussed nationally, including the prospect of nationalisation.

Regarding the amalgamation or nationalisation of the NSR, Lord Anslow, the chairman, remarked somewhat prophetically:

> In the interests of the district both for practical and sentimental reasons, we deprecate our Railway being obliterated from the map by being handed over to one of the neighbouring companies ... The loss to the district by removal of the Headquarters Staff, but the closure of the Locomotive, Carriage, and Waggon, Engineering and Electrical Works and by the cessation of purchase by the Railway Company in neighbourhood of their Stores, would mean, say £250,000 [loss] annually.
>
> (*Staffordshire Sentinel,* 13 February 1919)

At the next shareholders meeting, Lord Anslow opined that the NSR had been 'for a long time abused by a few cantankerous individuals whom nothing we did could please' and that in his twenty-seven years on the board he had never experienced anything similar. He bitterly opposed any move for amalgamation or nationalisation of the NSR.

Against this backdrop it was also reported that the NSR was paying a handsome dividend of 5 per cent to its shareholders (February 1919) and the train services were starting to return to normal. From 1 February 1919 'services will be greatly accelerated' and 'numerous additions and alterations' made on all lines. Clearly lessons from the

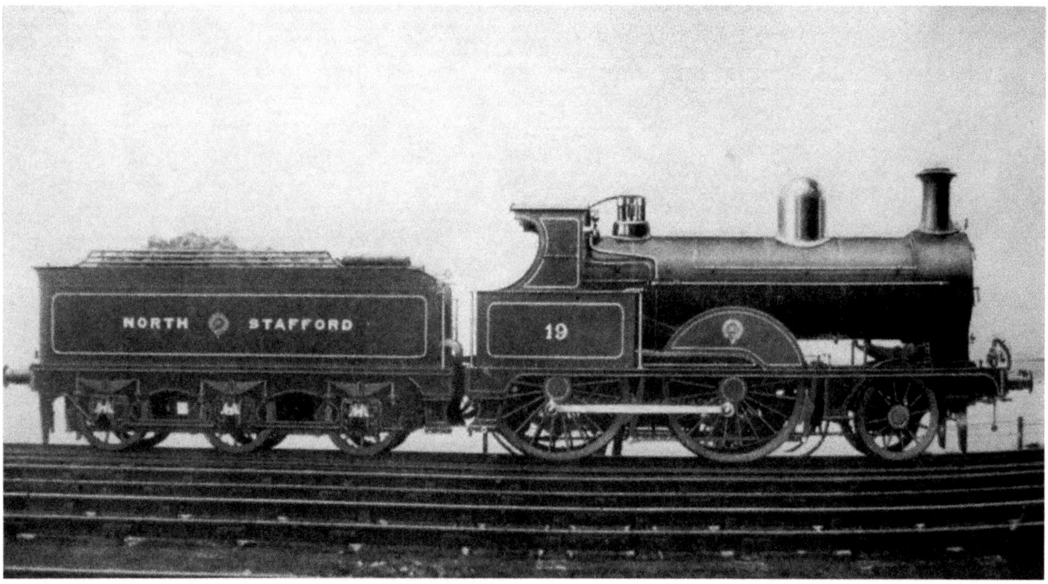

No. 19 was one of three '19' Class locomotives built at Stoke in 1905–06. They were the last 2-4-0 tender engines to be built in Britain. Of the trio, No. 15 was based at Stoke, No. 19 at Crewe and No. 54 at Uttoxeter for use on summer trains from Derby to North Wales. They were all withdrawn in 1920. (Foxfield Railway Museum)

drama of 1918–19 had been learned as in October 1919 a new timetable was introduced, all wartime restrictions were removed, services were accelerated and timings changed:

> Chiefly to meet the convenience of people returning home ... and to enable all passengers at all terminal stations to have every chance of reaching their destination. So far as the North Staffordshire Railway is concerned, every possible effort is being made in this direction.
>
> (*Staffordshire Sentinel*, 6 October 1919)

Special attention was also being paid to the goods service which were 'being resumed as rapidly as possible' and special arrangements made with the neighbouring companies for through traffic, especially of milk.

Redevelopment Plans

Following the turmoil of the war years and various Inquiries, the NSR had ambitious development and modernisation plans. A new electric power plant was started at Stoke and proposals were made to ease congestion around Hanley, Etruria and Newcastle-under-Lyme. An Act of 19 August 1921 allowed for the construction of a new double-track goods loop as well as diversion of the Ashbourne branch. New Up and Down marshalling yards were also planned between Newcastle Junction and Stoke and Stoke station was to be widened to provide four through roads.

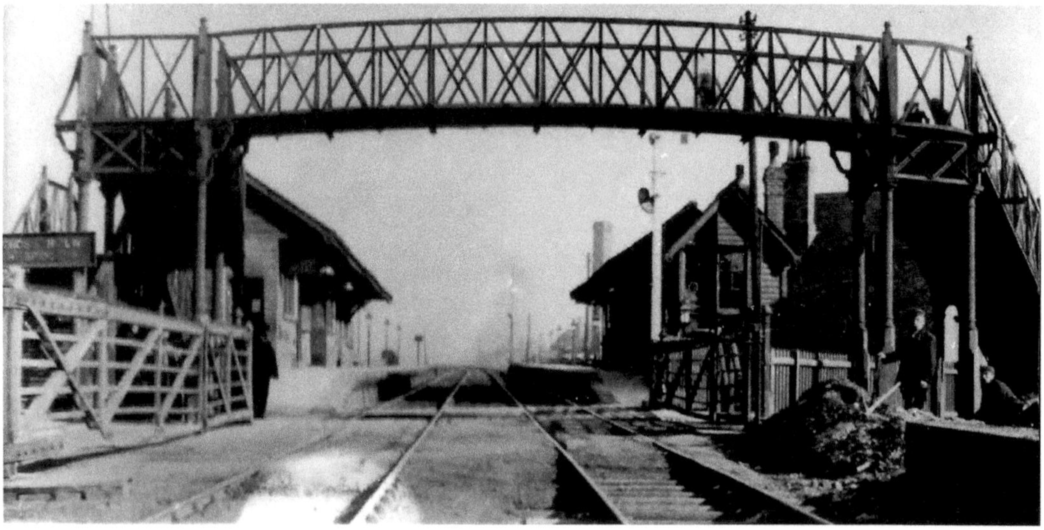

Fenton, on the Crewe–Derby line, opened in 1864, but the buildings were blown down in a gale in 1906 and replaced by new ones on a similar site. It closed in 1961. (Anthony Dawson)

In 1920, the NSR also purchased the Staffordshire Cricket Ground and in the following year formed an amateur athletic association. Sadly, 1920 also saw the closure of one of the oldest parts of the system: the Caldon Law inclines on 25 March.

One of the last gasps of the old Knotty came from Hookham at Stoke Works with the unique four-cylinder NSR No. 23. It was designed to work the intensive start-stop service on the steeply graded and tightly curved Potteries Loop Line so as to compete with encroaching tram and road services. The use of four cylinders was to give a high starting tractive effort but also an even torque to reduce hammer blow. It used four sets of Walschaerts valve gear. Sadly, the boiler was unable to meet demand from the cylinders and the water tanks and coal bunker were too small. Thus, she was rebuilt as a tender engine by the LMS in 1924 but being non-standard was scrapped at Crewe in 1928.

The NSR was also at the forefront of signalling and train control developments, carrying out trials in spring 1921 with the 'S.Y.X.' form of automatic train control developed by the W. R. Sykes Interlocking Signal Co. This was similar to that used by the GWR and used a metal ramp placed between the rails which raised a metal shoe fitted under the front end of the locomotive as it passed over. If the approaching distant signal was at 'Danger' the ramp was de-energised, but when it was set to 'All

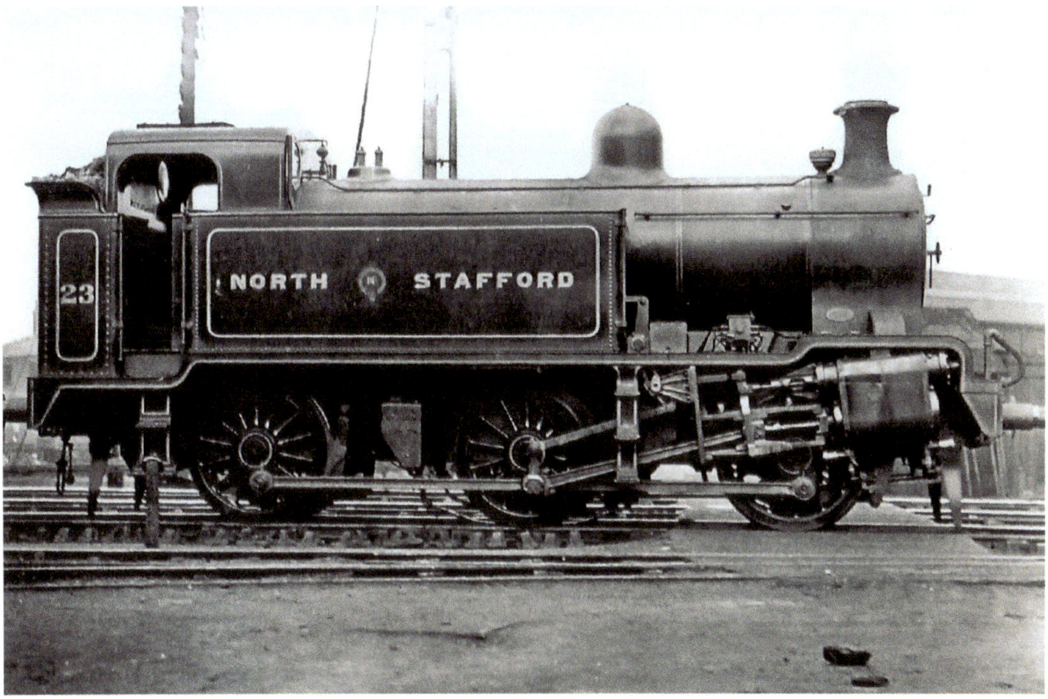

No. 23 was a unique four-cylinder locomotive design by Hookham to work the intensive passenger service on the steeply graded and sharply curved Potteries Loop Line. It was intended to have high power and speed between short station stops. A brave idea, but No. 23 was found less than satisfactory. (Foxfield Railway Museum)

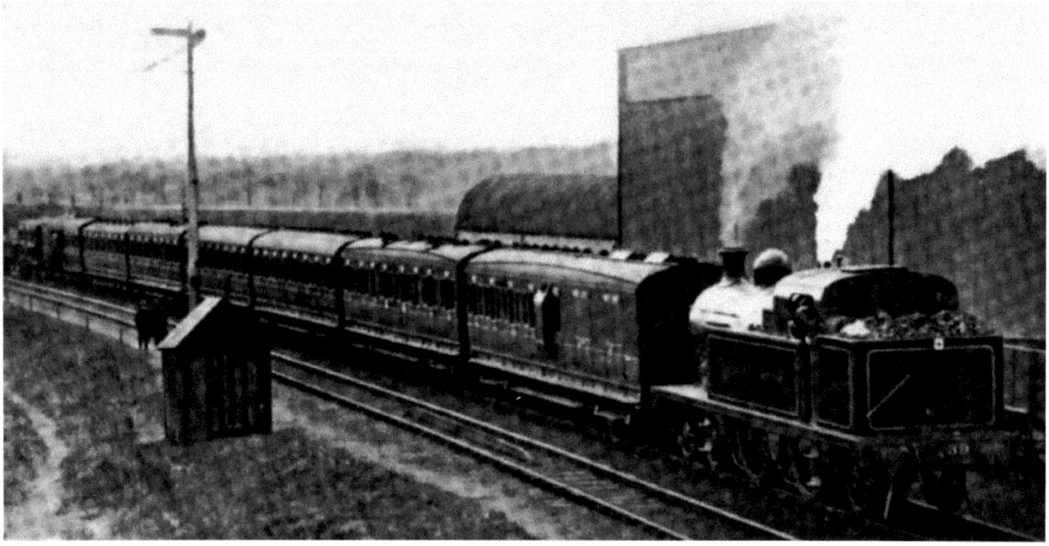

The NSR experimented with the 'S.Y.X.' form of automatic train control, and 'K' Class No. 39 was duly modified. Sadly, the introduction of the system was cancelled by the 'grouping' in 1923. (Foxfield Railway Museum)

Clear' it became energised, the current being picked up by the metal shoe. With the ramp de-energised, the lifting of the shoe opened a valve on the vacuum brake, and thus activated the train brakes while at the same time also applying the steam brake on the locomotive. The locomotive whistle was automatically sounded at the same time. Thus, if there were any failure of the electric current the 'Danger' signal would be given. If the signal were set to 'Clear' an electric bell would ring loudly in the cab – energised by the current picked up from the ramp. At the result of these tests it was recommended to adopt the system, but 'Grouping' got in the way.

5

Amalgamation and Rationalisation

Under the Auspices of the 1921 Railway Act the majority of Britain's railways were to be grouped into four major companies: the GWR, LNER, Southern and LMS, of which the NSR was to become part, taking sixth place in the new company which was then the largest joint-stock company in Britain. As Christiansen & Miller note, the NSR

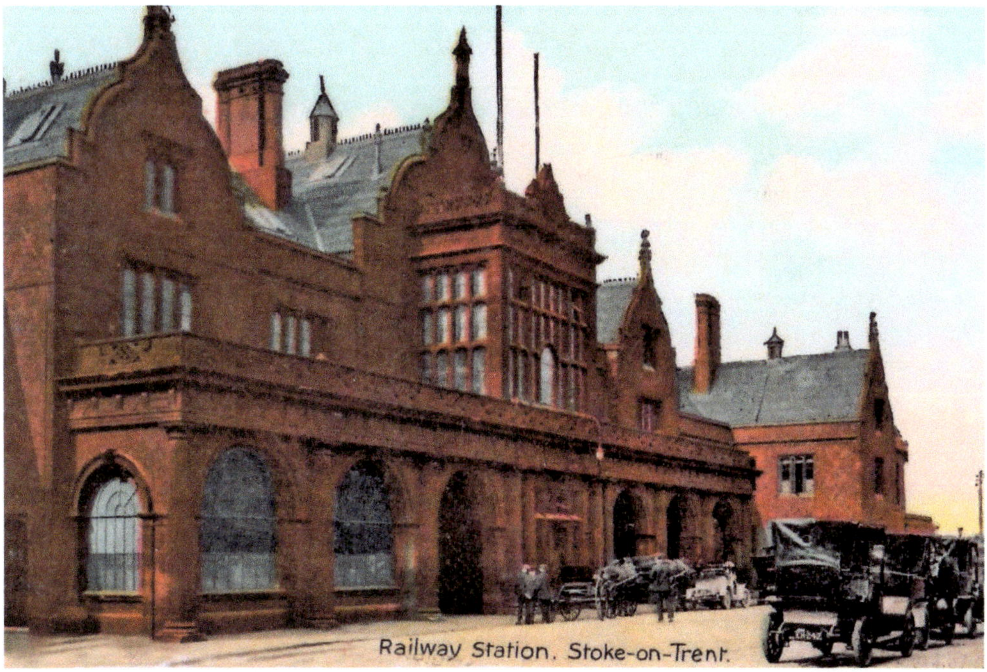

Stoke station, in a colourised postcard, *c.* 1925. (Foxfield Railway Museum)

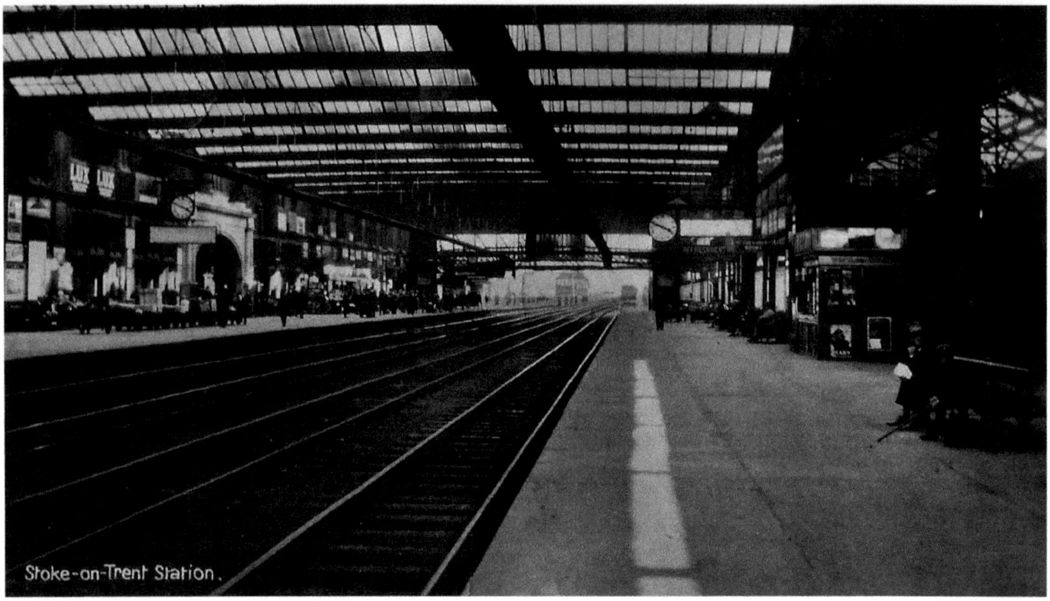

The interior of Stoke station, *c.* 1910 after the new overall roof was installed (1893), but before the opening of the new booking hall and NSR war memorial in 1923. (Foxfield Railway Museum)

'gave little to the LMS – and gained little from it'. However, although the LMS came into existence on 1 January 1923, the Knotty was independent to the end, holding out until 1 July 1923 due to various legal wranglings.

The announcement of grouping coincided with the remodelling of Stoke station to include a new entrance hall and booking offices, which incorporated the NSR's war memorial. The memorial was unveiled and dedicated on Tuesday 15 August 1922. A total of 1,423 of the company's employees (around 25 per cent) had served during the war. Bronze plaques on either side of the arch recorded 146 of those who lost their life during it; a further six names, curiously omitted in 1922, were added in 2017. The proceedings were opened by Major Wedgwood MP, who read each of the names of the fallen. He then invited the chairman, Lord Anslow, to unveil the memorial, who in his speech paid tribute to those who had died and also to the passing of the Knotty:

> There are great changes ahead of us, and the time is rapidly approaching when, for some of us, the close and intimate associations of many years may be broken up in the great amalgamation ... It was not of our seeking. It is to a great extent a sad but necessary consequence of the war. We can, however, confidently rely on North Staffordshire men and women, who follow after us, with reverent hearts and loving hands to watch over this memorial of gallant service...
>
> (*Staffordshire Advertiser*, 19 August 1922).

While the *Staffordshire Advertiser* (6 January 1923) used the opportunity to recount a history of the NSR, it welcomed grouping as the 'dawn of a new railway era', heralding 'a general lowering of the cost of travel and goods transport.... Passengers will gain immediate advantages by the availability of tickets ... Passengers will, for instance, be granted break of journey facilities on more than one route, where hitherto they have been prevented from breaking their journey except on a strictly defined route. In this way the travelling public will obtain the full advantage of combined rail services.'

The end of the NSR was marked by various dinners. A New Year dinner was held by the Railway Pensioners at the Stafford Railway Institute, which was attended by seventy retired employees of the NSR, LNWR and Great Northern. They had an average age of seventy-three and a combined service of 3,984 years. Toasts were proposed: 'Success to the London Midland & Scottish Railway.' More poignant were toasts to the LNWR and NSR, which prompted many stories and reminiscences from those present, including J. W. Dyson, who had worked for the LNWR for thirty-seven years and his father for forty-seven or Thomas Reynolds, a retired driver who had started railway work aged ten as a lad cleaner and retired aged seventy as the line's oldest driver, 'though he could have done a few more years'.

The NSR Police held its own dinner in Stoke, where the speaker, Mr. E. D. Grassett, traffic superintendent of the NS section of the LMS, recalled the loyalty of service of the NSR Police and hoped 'they would make their mark within the new group' and take a 'hopeful view of the future'. Sergeant E. Chappell, who had worked for the NSR for forty-five years, in proposing a toast for the senior officers remarked none of the NS men 'need never be ashamed of what they had accomplished'. In reply Mr Mather, Chief of the NSR Police, thanked all present for their service to the NSR and 'felt sure they would hold their own with any other Railway Police in the United Kingdom'.

The passing of the Knotty may not have been mourned by the general public. The inquiry (and its fallout) from 1918–19 was perhaps still fresh in the mind, but also concern about the Potteries Tramway Bill, which would give the Potteries Electric Traction Co. an absolute monopoly on road transport in North Staffordshire, running a road bus and motor car service alongside its electric trams. Stoke Corporation, and public opinion, was unanimously opposed. The Potteries, however, lost its electric trams in 1928, when motor buses won the day. In 1933, the PET was renamed Potteries Motor Traction.

LMS Reductions

Almost immediately the LMS began a policy of reductions. One of the first of which was the cessation of locomotive building at Stoke Works. The last four locomotives, a batch of New L Class (Nos 1, 2, 10 and 48) were the last to be completed. They were turned out in full NSR livery. The works were closed on 31 December 1926. The run

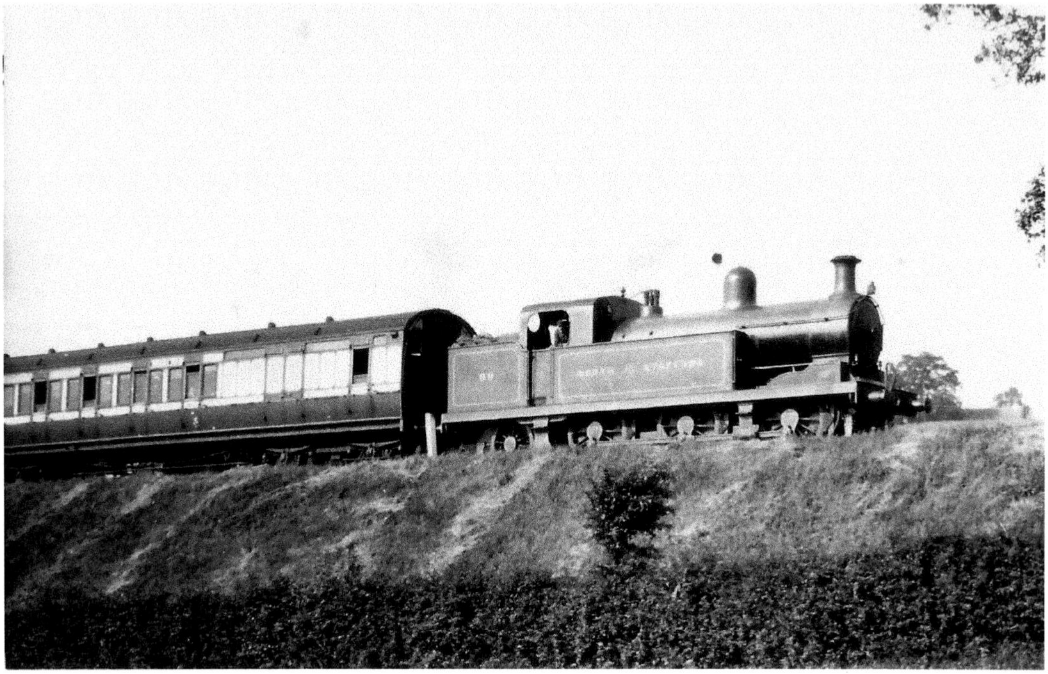

'New L' Class No. 99 with a train of NSR bogie stock near Derby in 1923. (Foxfield Railway Museum)

down continued until July 1927 and the staff were encouraged to take up employment at either Crewe or Derby. Indeed, a special train was introduced between Stoke and Crewe and a special halt opened alongside Crewe Works to cater for staff who resided in Stoke.

The closure of Stoke Works coincided with the LMS reorganising and rationalising its sheds. Stoke and other depots all became No. 40. Things changed again in 1933 with the introduction of numbers and letters to identify sheds. Three ex-NSR sheds were included in the Crewe district – Stoke (5D), Alsager (5E) and Uttoxeter (5F). Macclesfield (9) came under the auspices of Manchester Longsight. Where sheds were duplicated, the NSR sheds were invariably closed. Those at Crewe and Burton-upon-Trent closed shortly after grouping, so too the NSR sheds at Derby and Colwich. Further economies saw Market Drayton shed close in April 1931, Leek Brook in January 1932 and Ashbourne in November 1932.

The LMS also began withdrawing NSR locomotives as it was not considered economic to maintain small classes of non-standard locomotives. The New L Class 0-6-2Ts were considered sufficiently successful. The LMS put some examples to work as far afield as Bradford in West Yorkshire and St Pancras in London, for which purpose several were modified with cut-down boiler mountings, cabs and radiused buffer beams to work on the former Midland underground lines. Two

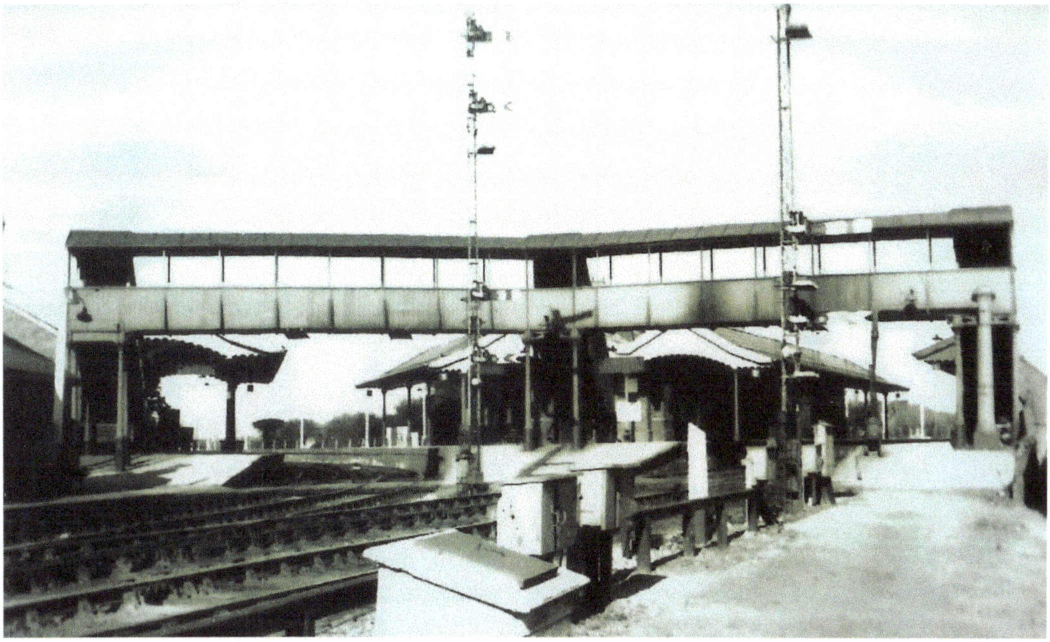

The present Uttoxeter station came into use in October 1881. Prior to that there had been three separate stations: the first Uttoxeter Bridge Street (1848), Uttoxeter Junction (1849) and Uttoxeter Dove Bank (1849). (Anthony Dawson)

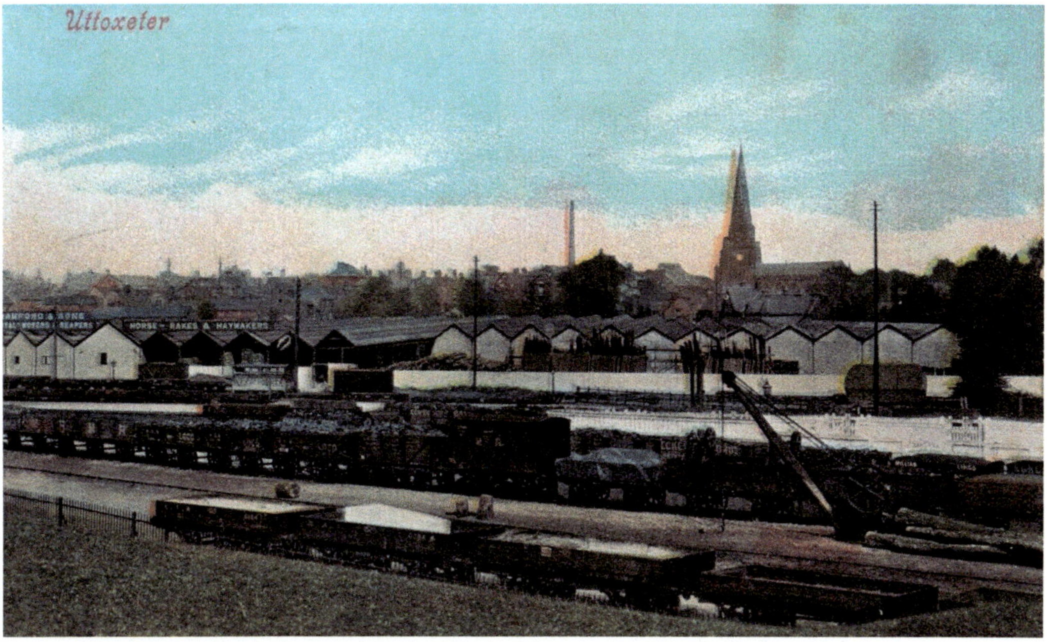

Uttoxeter once had an extensive goods yard, handling traffic from the Crewe–Derby line, and Churnet Valley Line. (Anthony Dawson)

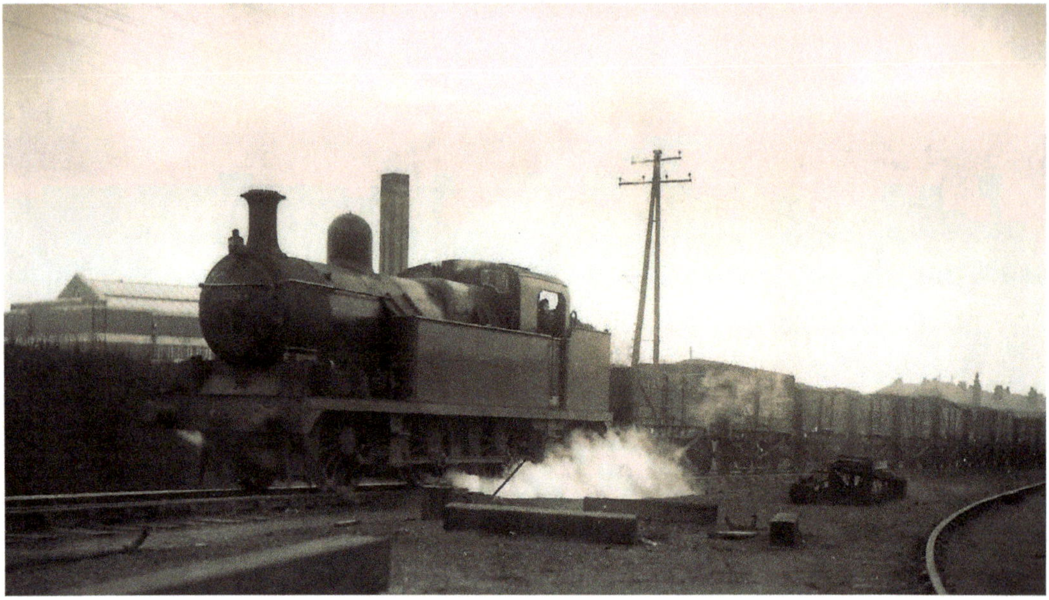

'New L' Class No. 2 was one of five sold to the Walkden Collieries, Manchester, in the 1930s. Seen here still carrying its LMS number 2271. (Foxfield Railway Museum)

were transferred to Manchester Longsight to work the Manchester, South Junction & Altrincham Railway, replacing the elderly LNWR Coal tanks hitherto used on the intensely worked system. So successful were the New Ls that had it not been for the success of Henry Fowler's 2-6-2Ts they would have become a standard class on the LMS. In 1936, one of them was sold to the Longmoor Military Railway and five were sold to the Manchester Collieries Ltd at Walkden, of which NSR No. 2 was selected to be repainted in full NSR livery at Crewe Works for public display at Stoke in 1960 to mark the jubilee of the city of Stoke-on-Trent. It later returned to the colliery but was rebuilt in 1964. The boiler, cab, tank and bunker from No. 2 were put on the frames and wheels of NSR No. 72, creating a hybrid locomotive. NSR No. 69 went on to become the last NSR engine at work. Renamed *Robert* and repainted in NSR livery in August 1965, it was withdrawn in 1969 and tragically scrapped in September. Happily, No. 2 was acquired for preservation by Staffordshire Museums and put on display at Shugborough Hall. Since 2016 it has been on display at the Foxfield Railway.

There were changes in the coaching stock too. The last four wheelers were swept away, as were the oldest of the six wheelers and in total one-third of all Knotty coaching stock was withdrawn. Probably the last six-wheel coach was withdrawn as late as 1953 in South Wales, having been built as long ago as 1905. Two seven-coach sets of NSR bogie coaches were still in use at Uttoxeter until 1953, and the last two NSR coaches lasted until 1958.

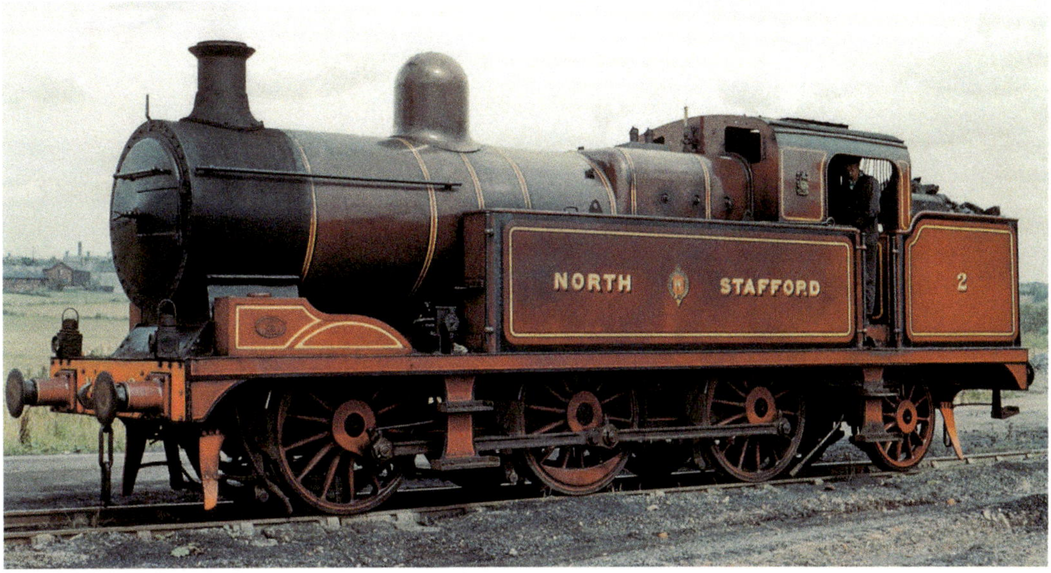

No. 2 was restored to her original NSR livery by Crewe works for the jubilee celebrations of the city of Stoke-on-Trent in May 1960. No. 2 still carries this paint work to this day – and must have looked somewhat incongruous working at Walkden Collieries in NSR livery! (Foxfield Railway Museum)

Line Closures

Under the LMS there followed the usual pattern of closures and withdrawals of service. One of the first NSR branches, the Biddulph Valley, lost its passenger service on 11 July 1927, the line having long been unremunerative. The stations were poorly sited, but as a mineral line it was still very important. The Trentham branch was closed to local services in September 1927, but was to remain open for excursions. The Sandbach branch lost its passenger service on 28 July 1930 and passenger services on the Audley line – once one of the busiest on the NSR – ceased on 27 April 1931 ,and the Talke Branch was partially closed in the same year.

The loss of passenger services on the Audley line paved the way for others, such as the Market Drayton line, which was closed on 27 April 1931. The section between Silverdale and Pipe Gate was singled in 1934, with Pipe Gate continuing to handle race day specials for Keele Park. Not everything was cost-cutting and retrenchment, however. The tunnel on the Cheadle branch, which had always proved troublesome (indeed 400 feet of the roof collapsed in 1918), was eliminated by the opening of a deviation on 26 November 1933.

Another victim of the LMS regime was the Leek & Manifold. The LMS had not wanted to acquire the loss-making little line, but had been forced to purchase it for £30,000 by Parliament. It was closed on 12 March 1934, which in turn 'took the legs

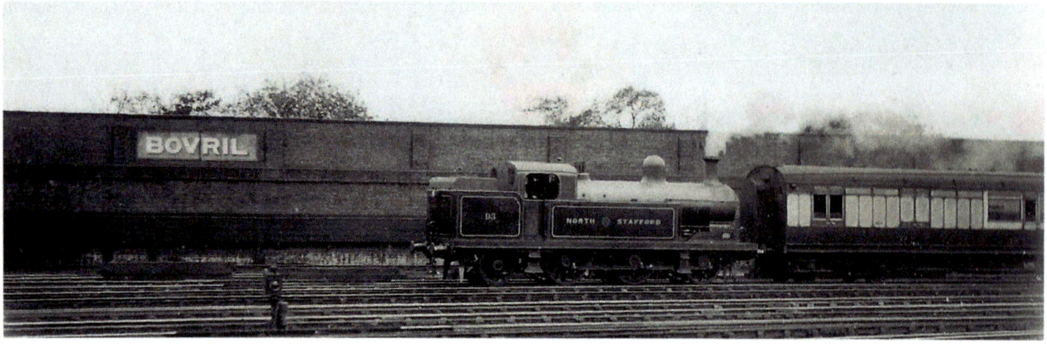

'New L' Class No. 63 approaches Crewe with a train of NSR bogie carriages *c.* 1920. No. 93 was one of the original eight engines built with a round-top firebox in 1909. Seen here converted for oil firing. (Foxfield Railway Museum)

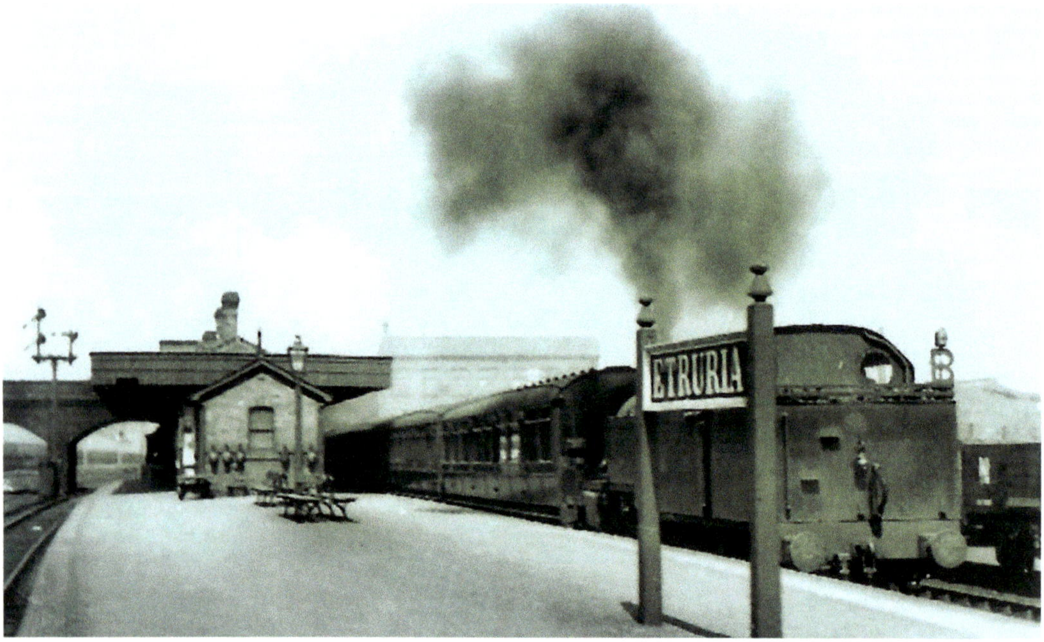

Etruria station in pre-war LMS days. The Etruria station seat was latterly preserved at Foxfield. (Anthony Dawson)

from under the Leek-Waterhouses passenger services', which finished at the end of the 1935 summer season on 30 September 1935. There was, however, considerable controversy over the Manifold line's future. The LMS put the track bed up for sale and local councils wanted it, converting into a road. In opposition were ramblers and walking groups, who pressed for the railway to be converted into a footpath. They won the day, and the popular Manifold Way walking route was opened in July 1937.

Enter British Railways

One of the first effects of nationalisation in 1948 was the closure of several offices in Stoke, including the North Staffordshire district engineer, bringing to an end over a century of tradition. Having been losing on average £16,000 a year, trains were withdrawn between Uttoxeter, Ashbourne and Buxton on 1 November 1954. This is not surprising, however, given that the average number of passengers was only nineteen. Two big cuts came two years later when passenger services were withdrawn between Silverdale and Market Drayton, and Stoke and Leek on 7 May 1956, saving over £6,000 per year.

The Burton–Tutbury branch, known and loved locally as the 'Tutbury Jennie', lost its local passenger service on 13 June 1960 despite hopes the line would be dieselised. In fact, closure had been on the cards since the mid-1930s, but the Second World War had saved it. During 1932 the branch was used to trial a Sentinel-Cammell steam rail car capable of carrying forty-four passengers, and four years later a diesel-electric rail car with accommodation for fifty-three passengers. The branch had been losing money at £7,300 per year and thanks to increased car ownership, high fares, and poor service, only carrying on a dozen passengers per day. Even more dramatic was the loss of passenger services on the Churnet Valley line on 5 November 1960. And like the loss of the Tutbury service, there was plenty of objection. The trains were said

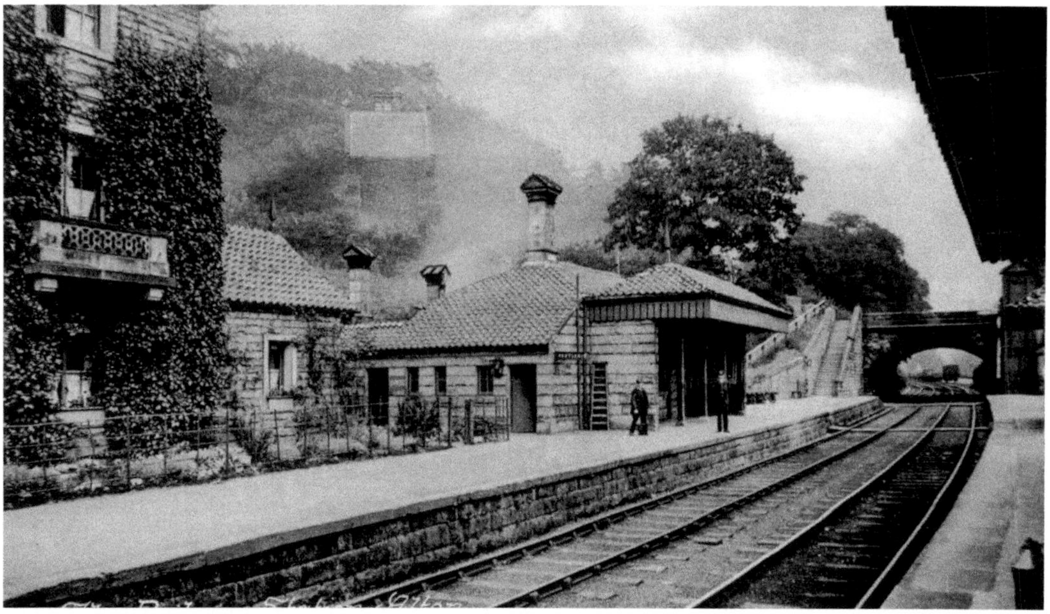

Alton station on the Churnet Valley Line seen in its glory days of the Edwardian period. It was renamed Alton Towers in 1954. Following closure of the line, the station buildings were acquired by the Landmark Trust and the stationmasters house is now a holiday let. (Anthony Dawson)

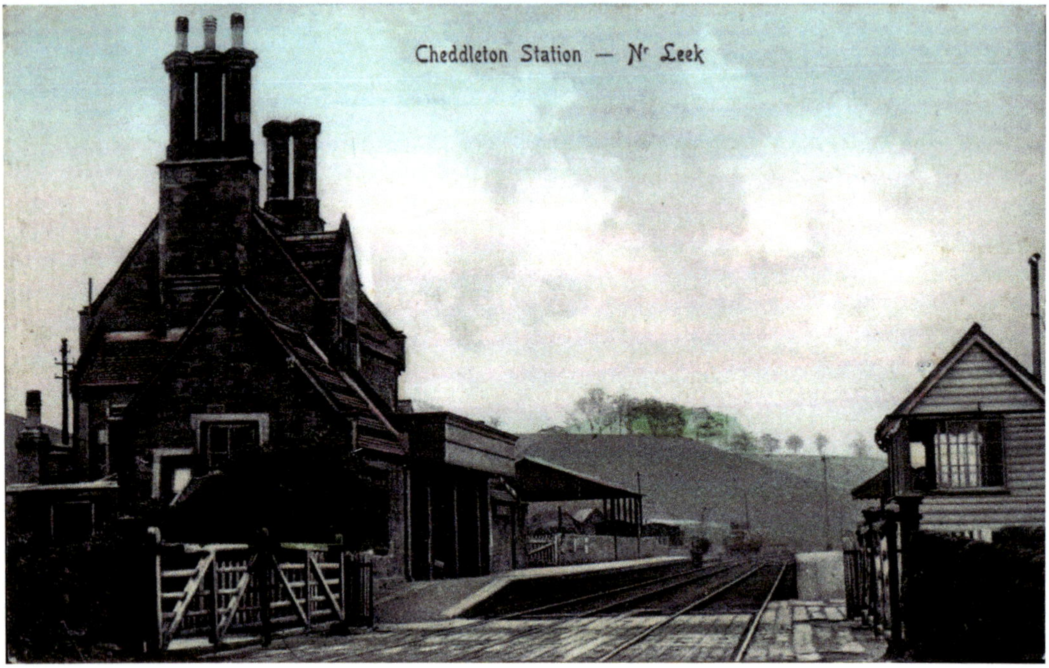

Cheddleton Station on the Churnet Valley Line closed in 1965, but thanks to the efforts of preservationists is now HQ of the Churnet Valley Railway heritage line. (Anthony Dawson)

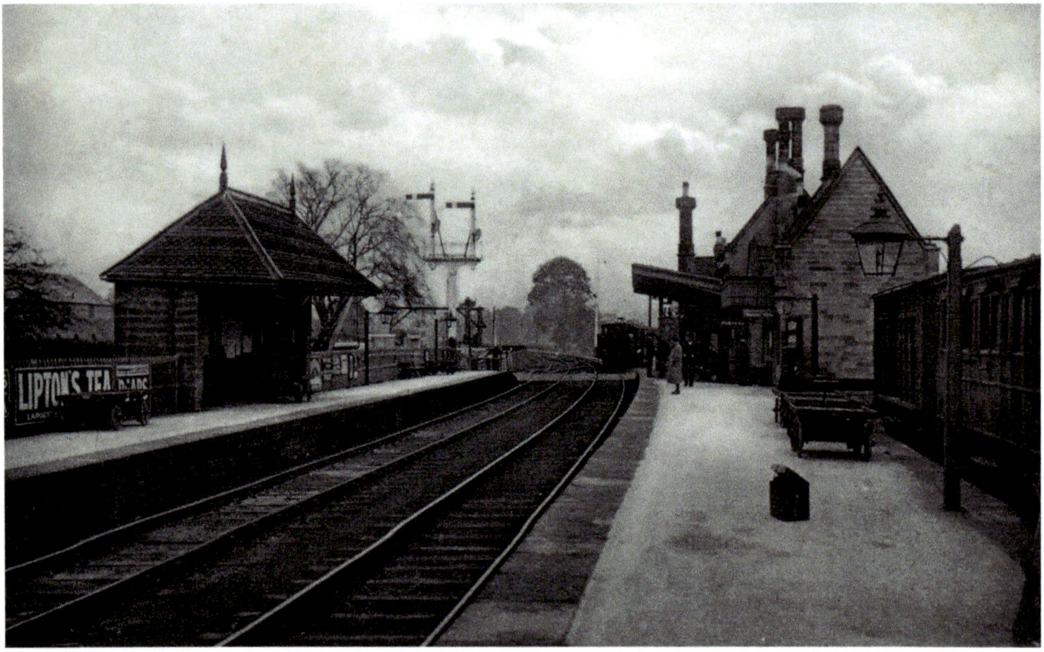

Another loss with the closer of the Churnet Valley Line was Rocester. It opened in 1849 and three years later became a junction when the NSR built a branch to Ashbourne. Passenger services ended as early as 1954 and goods in 1964. (Anthony Dawson)

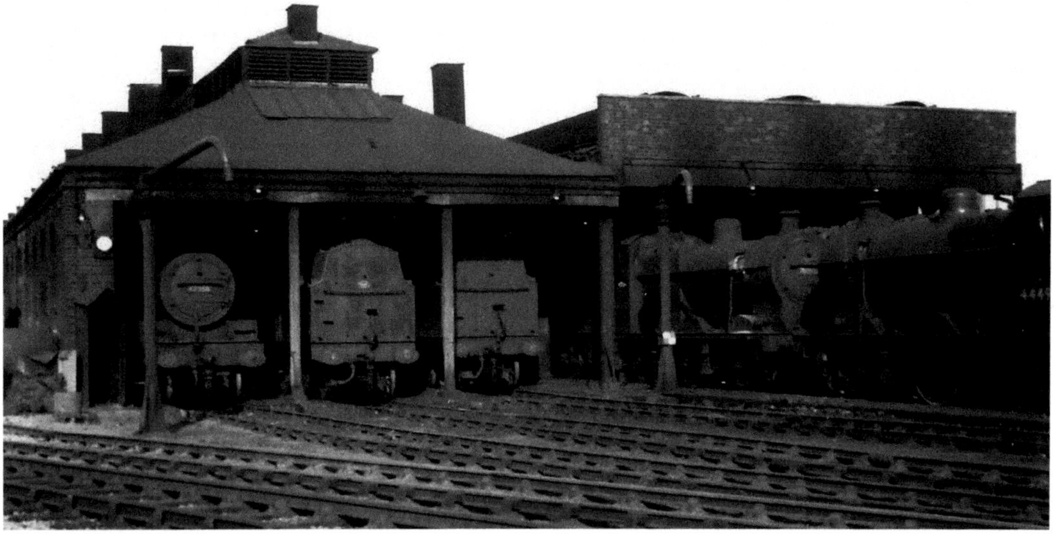

Stoke Shed 30 September 1956. On shed are a pair of Fowler 4F 0-6-0s (including 44496) and three Fowler 4P 2-6-4 tanks including 42398. (Anthony Dawson)

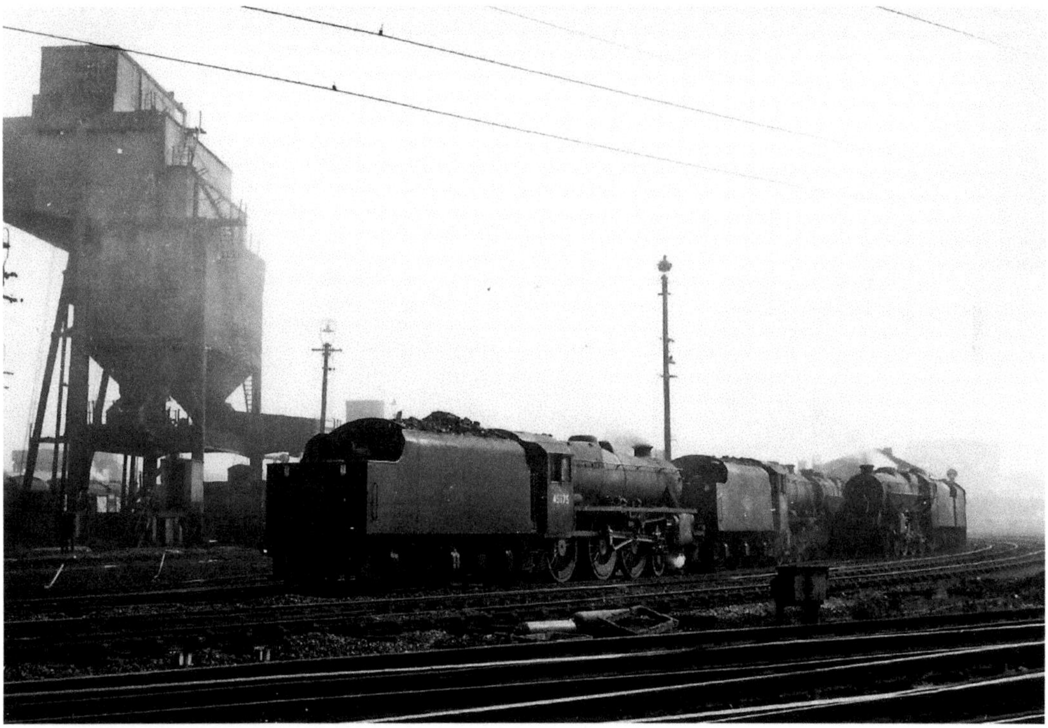

A group of LMS Black Fives wait near the Stoke coaling stage. No. 45375 was built by Armstrong Whitworth in 1937 and allocated to Stoke in October 1961. It was scrapped in 1967. (Anthony Dawson)

to be losing £22,000 a year and that the area would be just as well served by buses. The section from Oakamoor to Uttoxeter officially closed on 4 January 1965. The last pre-Beeching closure was the Audley branch from which goods traffic was withdrawn from 7 January 1963, some thirty-two years after regular passenger services had ceased. Regular goods workings had not used the line for about two years.

Alongside these closures came modernization, with diesels beginning to replace steam from 1956 when Derby 'lightweight' DMUs began operating on Macclesfield, Bollington & Marple. A large diesel maintenance depot was opened at Cockshutt sidings, Stoke, in December 1957 capable of servicing thirty-eight DMUs a day. Diesels were introduced between Stoke and Manchester on 3 March 1958, worked by sets based at Stoke and Buxton.

The Beeching Report

The Beeching Report of 27 March 1963 included the closure of many former NSR lines. The Leek–Uttoxeter service was slated for withdrawal, together with the Potteries Loop Line, the Stoke–Silverdale stub of the Market Drayton line, and the MB&M services to Manchester. Passenger services on the Cheadle line were also to be withdrawn, which happened on 17 June 1963. The southern section of the L&GBR closed in December

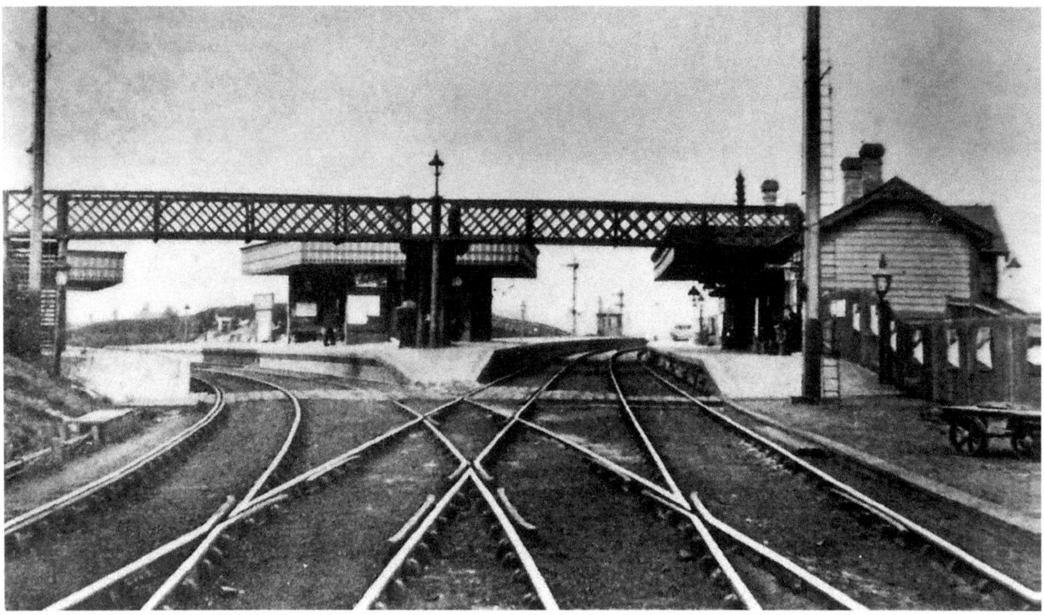

Harecastle, nowadays Kidsgrove, on the Crewe–Derby line was opened in October 1848 and has been variously known as Harecastle Junction, Kidsgrove Junction, Harecastle (1875), Harecastle for Kidsgrove (1885–86 and 1923–24), and simply Kidsgrove from 1944. (Anthony Dawson)

1963 and the northern section in July the following year. Goods traffic on the Cheadle Branch was withdrawn in 1978, and the line remained open for a small amount of civil engineering traffic until November 1984. The Market Drayton branch was axed in March 1966 with Newcastle-under-Lyme, one of the largest towns in the area, losing its rail service. Other economies were made at the Burton end of the line, including on the Tutbury branch and between Stretton and Egginton Junction. The MB&M finally closed in 1970, other than a mile-long stretch from Rose Hill Marple to Marple Wharf Junction providing a connection to Manchester Piccadilly.

However, it was not all doom and gloom. Finally, thanks to electrification of the West Coast Mainline, Stoke would get the mainline express trains that the NSR promoters had desired back in the 1840s when many of the London–Manchester expresses were routed through Stoke. Indeed, the platforms at Stoke were lengthened to handle twelve-coach trains but one of the through roads was removed to provide space for the overhead line equipment. Part of this scheme involved the creation of a £1 million project to divert the mainline away from the old Harecastle Tunnels, which opened in June 1966. Electric services were introduced from 2 January 1967, initially to steam timings, but from 6 March they were upgraded with high-speed services. Macclesfield Hibel Road was closed in November 1960 and trains diverted into the present Macclesfield Central. A new freight terminal was opened in Stoke in May 1961 at a cost of £750,000.

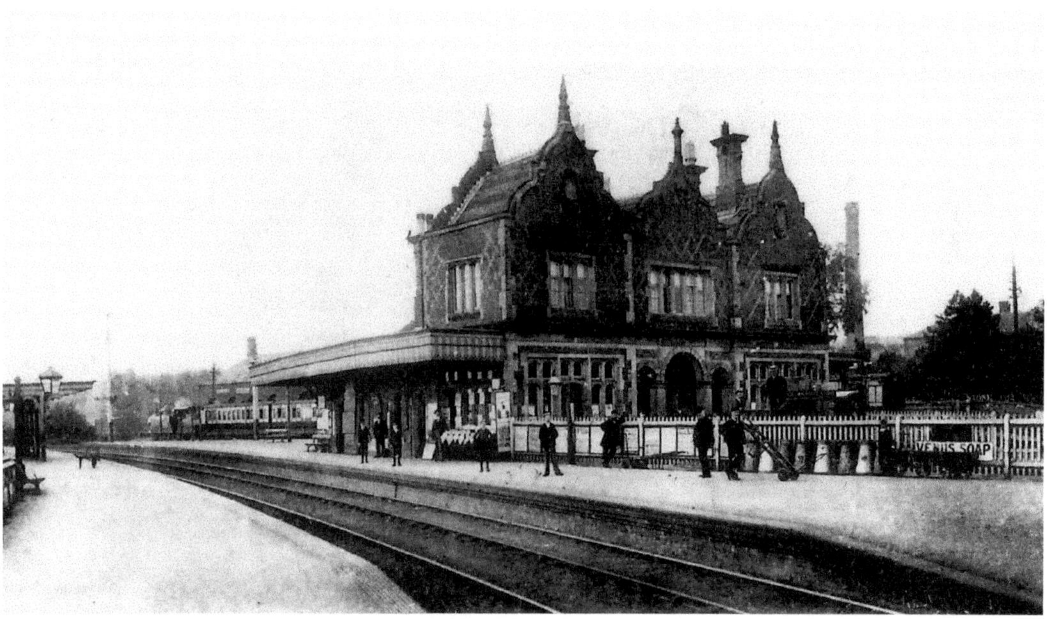

Stone possesses one of the most magnificent neo-Jacobean station buildings on the NSR, opening in 1849 to the design of Sir Henry Arthur Hunt. Passenger services were withdrawn in 2004 but reinstated during 2008. (Anthony Dawson)

6

The Knotty Preserved

Although the Knotty died a century ago, the NSR is alive and well. Perhaps the longest lasting legacy is Stoke-on-Trent station and Winton Square, which has some of the finest railway architecture in the country and quite rightly is Grade II* listed. There is a flourishing NSR study group, but the traditions of the Knotty are carried on by two heritage railways: the Foxfield and the Churnet Valley railways and the narrow-gauge Rudyard Lake Railway. The Knotty is perhaps the only railway in the world to have had a play written about it, performed at the Victoria Theatre, Stoke, in July and August 1966. It was so popular it was revived in October 1967 and again in 1969.

The Foxfield Railway began life as a narrow-gauge railway but was rebuilt to standard gauge in 1893 to carry coal from Foxfield Colliery to exchange sidings on the Stoke–Uttoxeter line at Blythe Bridge. Engineered by Donald Munro, a Scottish civil engineer with an office in Manchester, the Foxfield line was built using second-hand NSR materials by NSR platelayers supervised by NSR foreman platelayer Noah Stanyer at the weekend. When the colliery closed in 1965, preservationists almost immediately moved in. The colliery had been purchased by Tean Minerals Ltd as a mineral-processing plant, and two of the senior managers were steam enthusiasts. It was intended to use the moribund colliery line to carry mineral products for Tean Minerals during the week, with the enthusiasts running steam trains at the weekend and also maintaining the track. The inaugural meeting of the Foxfield Light Railway Society was held in February 1967. Its first locomotive, *Henry Cort*, arrived from Irthlingborough Ironstone Quarry in the same month, and the first passenger train, consisting of *Henry Cort* and *Marston, Thompson & Evershed No. 3* topping-and-tailing an LMS coach, travelled on the Foxfield Railway on 14 May 1967. The railway's present HQ at Caverswall Road opened at Easter 1982 and there is much NSR infrastructure in evidence, such as the 1895 Mackenzie & Holland signal box from Hockley Crossing as well as NSR No. 2. The present station building was completed in 1995 in NSR style and incorporates cast-iron canopy columns from the demolished Blythe Bridge station. The museum also displays several NSR items as well as components from the Consall and Caldon Low plateways.

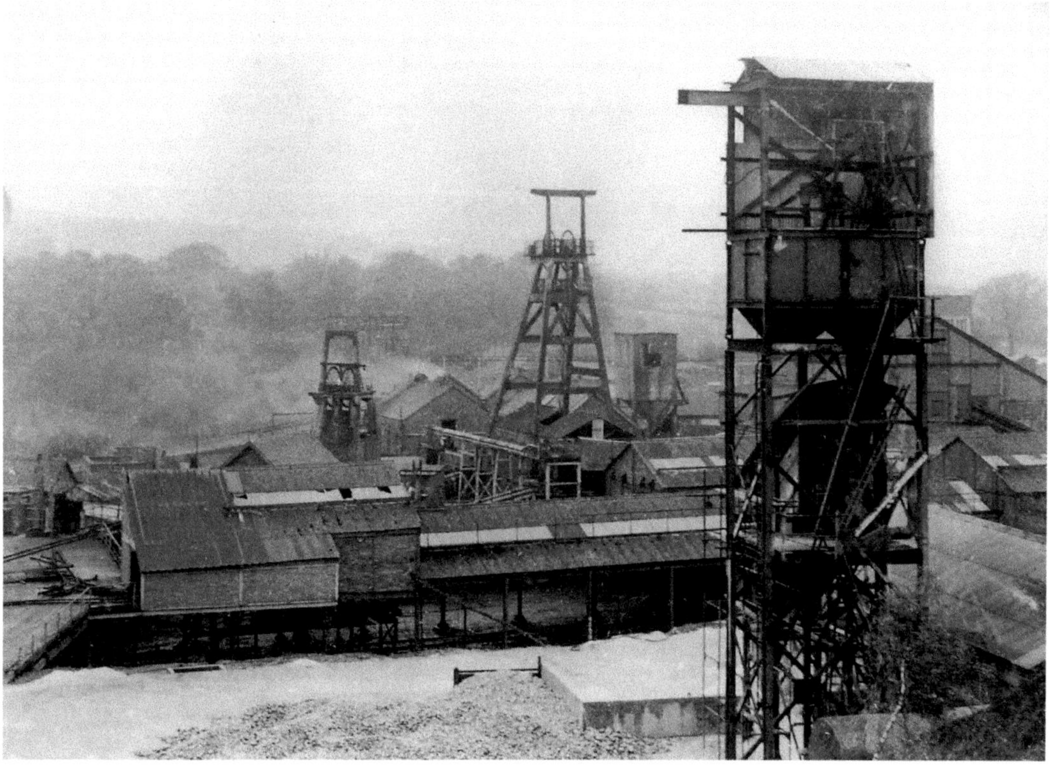

The first shaft of the Foxfield Colliery was sunk in April 1880 by John and Enoch Mann. It is seen here two years after closure in May 1967. (Foxfield Railway Museum)

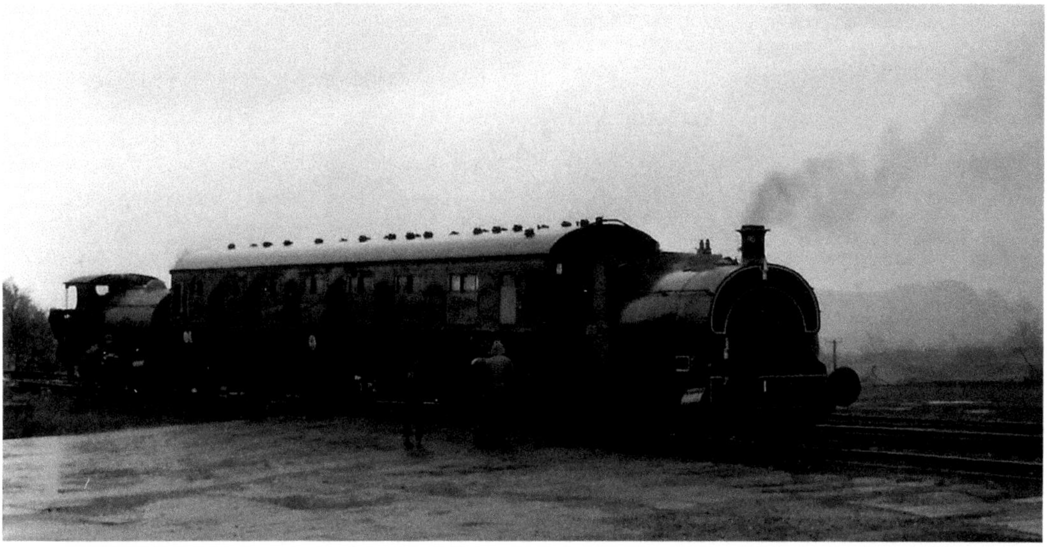

The first passenger train of the preservation era departed Foxfield Colliery on 14 May 1967 the single coach hauled by *Henry Cort* and *Marston*. (Anthony Dawson)

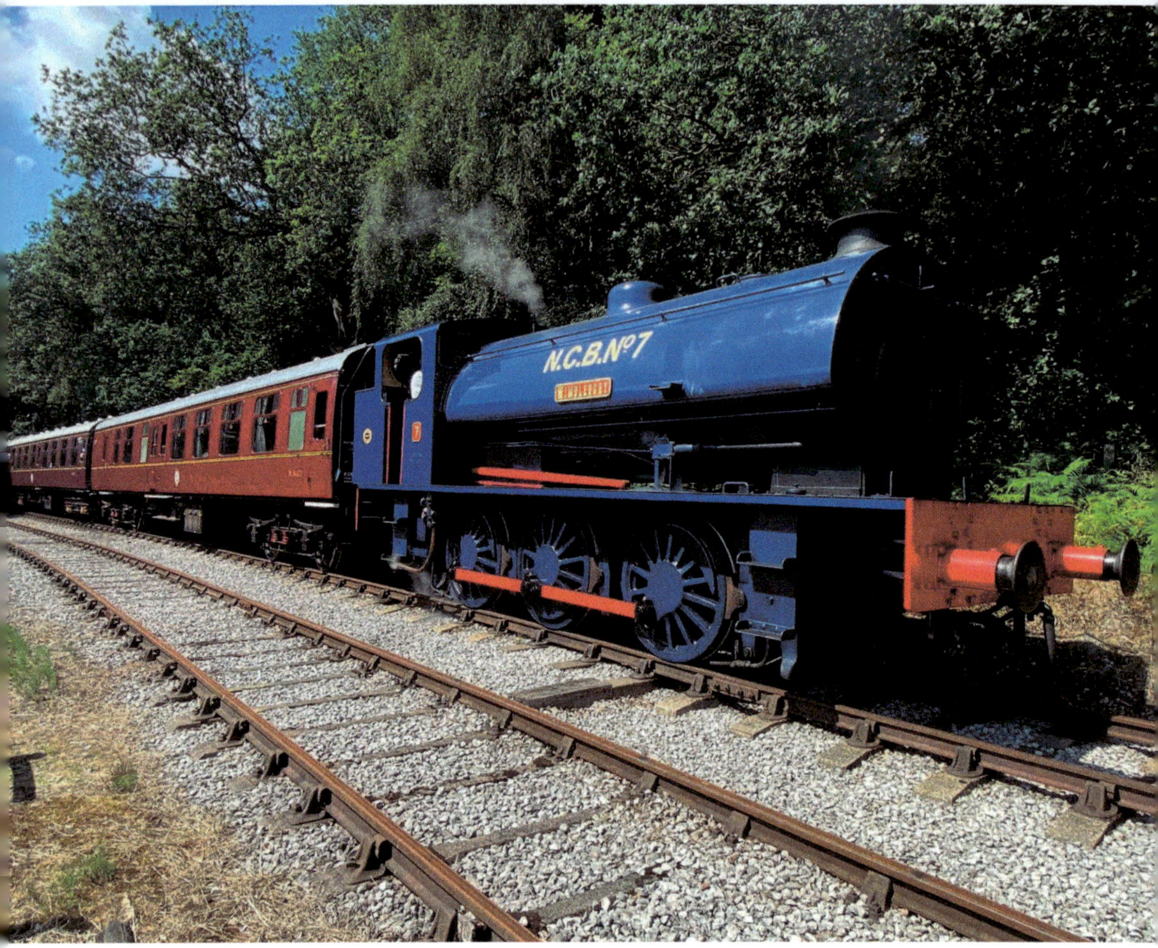

Foxfield today is a flourishing heritage railway. Hunslet 'Austerity' *Wimblebury* heads a trio of BR Mark 1 carriages. (Kieron Rigby)

Foxfield is also home of the Knotty Coach Trust, formed to restore NSR Victorian wooden-bodied coaches. At present the trust operates three Victorian four-wheelers: NSR third class No. 61, probably built in 1876 at Stoke. It was withdrawn from service around 1910 and the body used a platelayer's hut at Tutbury station, eventually becoming a garden shed. It was rescued in 1976 by the Foxfield Railway, who undertook a partial restoration. It was fully restored and returned to service in the 1990s. NSR third-class No. 127 was built in the mid-1880s. Withdrawn around 1907, it found its way to the Leek & Manifold Railway as a waiting room. It was moved to Ecton when the L&MVR closed in the 1930s and donated to Foxfield in 1980 and was restored to service in the 2000s. Finally there is NSR brake-third No. 23, which was found as a complete wreck at Rudyard Lake with the remains of several others. It was restored by Stanegate Restorations, including disabled access, and entered traffic in

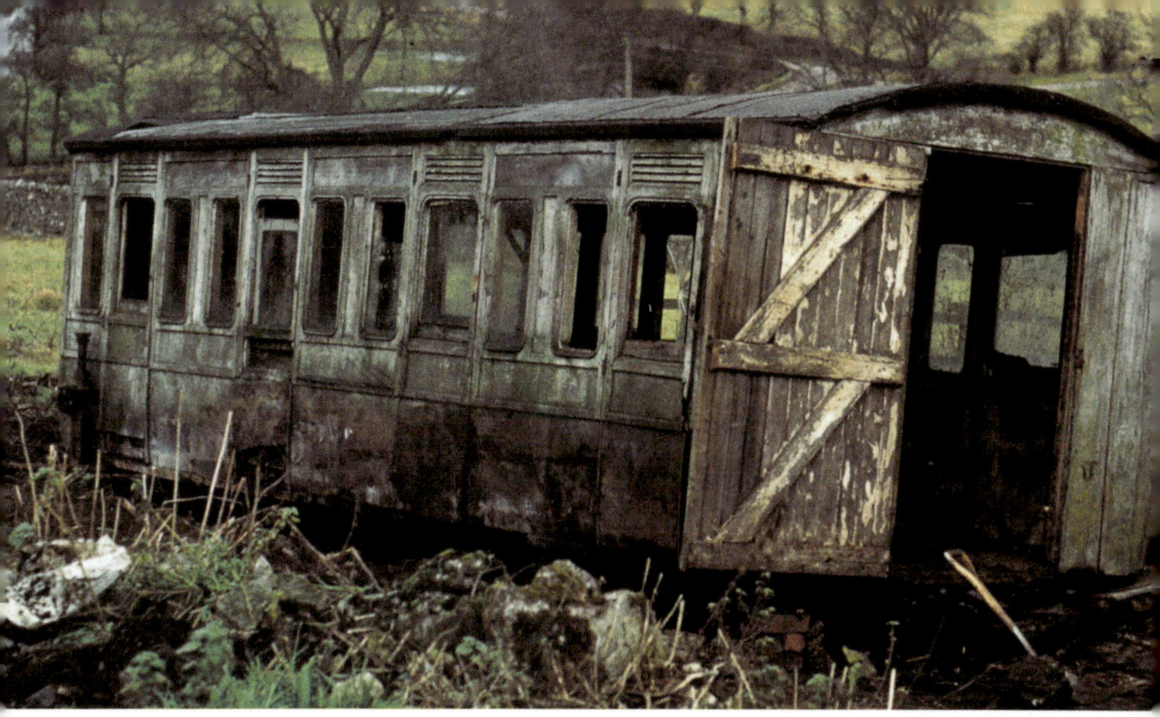

Before: The body of NSR third-class four-wheeler No. 127 in a field in Ecton (Knotty Coach Trust)

2019. The Knotty Coach Trust also own an NSR brake van as well as first-class carriage, both awaiting their turn for restoration.

While Foxfield is full of NSR ambience, the Churnet Valley runs on a part of the NSR route and indeed has magnificent NSR buildings. Opened in October 1996, it originated as the Cheshire and Staffordshire Railway Society, which had the original idea of saving some or all of the Biddulph Valley Line, but this was met with only a lukewarm response by the local authorities. Attention then turned to a section of the Churnet Valley line from Oakamoor to Alton Towers, with HQ at Cheddleton – it was only thanks to local opposition, including one parish councillor parking his car on the level crossing in front of bulldozers, which allowed the building to be listed and gain reprieve. The station and sidings at Cheddleton were purchased in 1977 and in the following year the North Staffordshire Railway (1978) was formed. BR ceased using the Churnet Valley line for stone trains in 1988, and the tracked from Oakamoor to Leek Brook Junction was purchased in 1992. Trains began running in 1996, which in 2022 operated between Leek Brook and Kingsley & Froghall.

Also operating on former NSR trackbed is the Rudyard Lake Railway, a 10.25-inch-gauge line, which uses miniature locomotives on 1½ miles of the former NSR route, beginning life in 1985.

Th'owd Knotty lives on too in the novels of Arnold Bennett, who immortalised the Potteries and NSR in his writing.

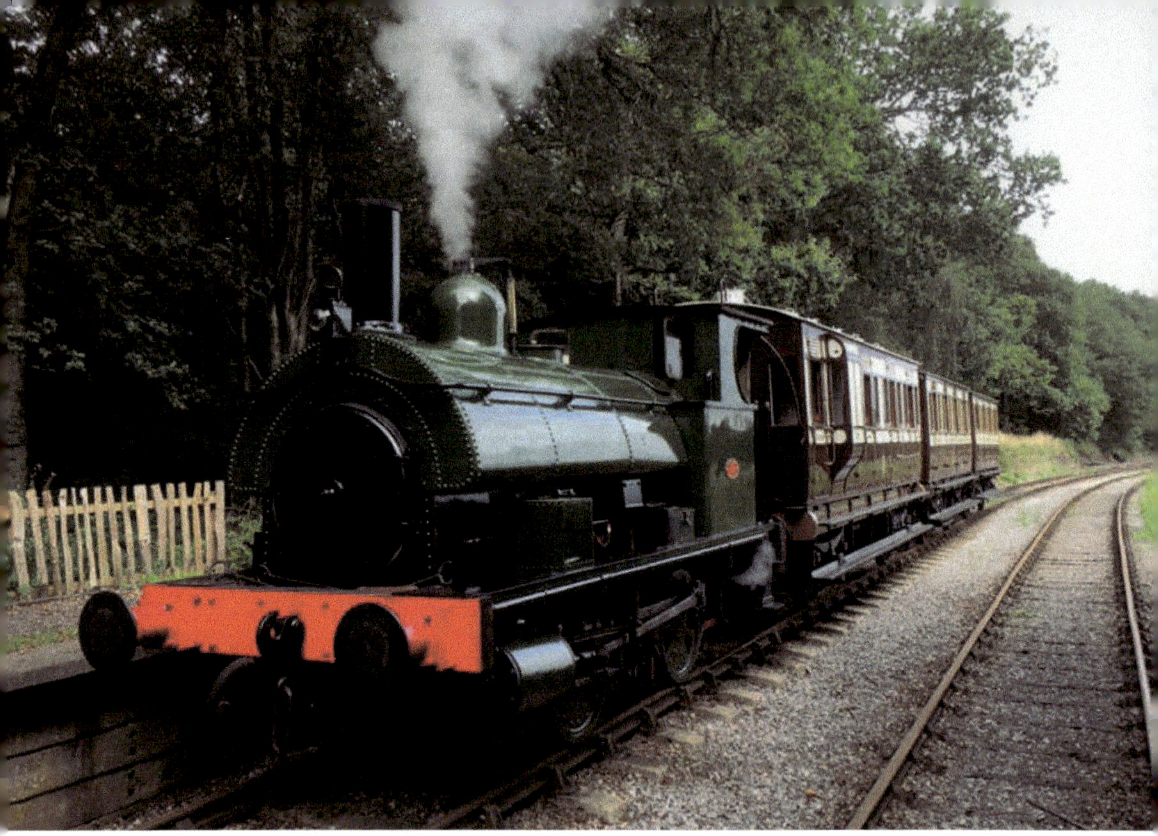

Above: After: Restored train of three four-wheel NSR carriages in use on the Foxfield Railway, hauled by Beyer Peacock No. 1827 of 1878. (Nigel Brazier/Knotty Coach Trust)

Below: Cheddleton, HQ of the restored Churnet Valley Railway.

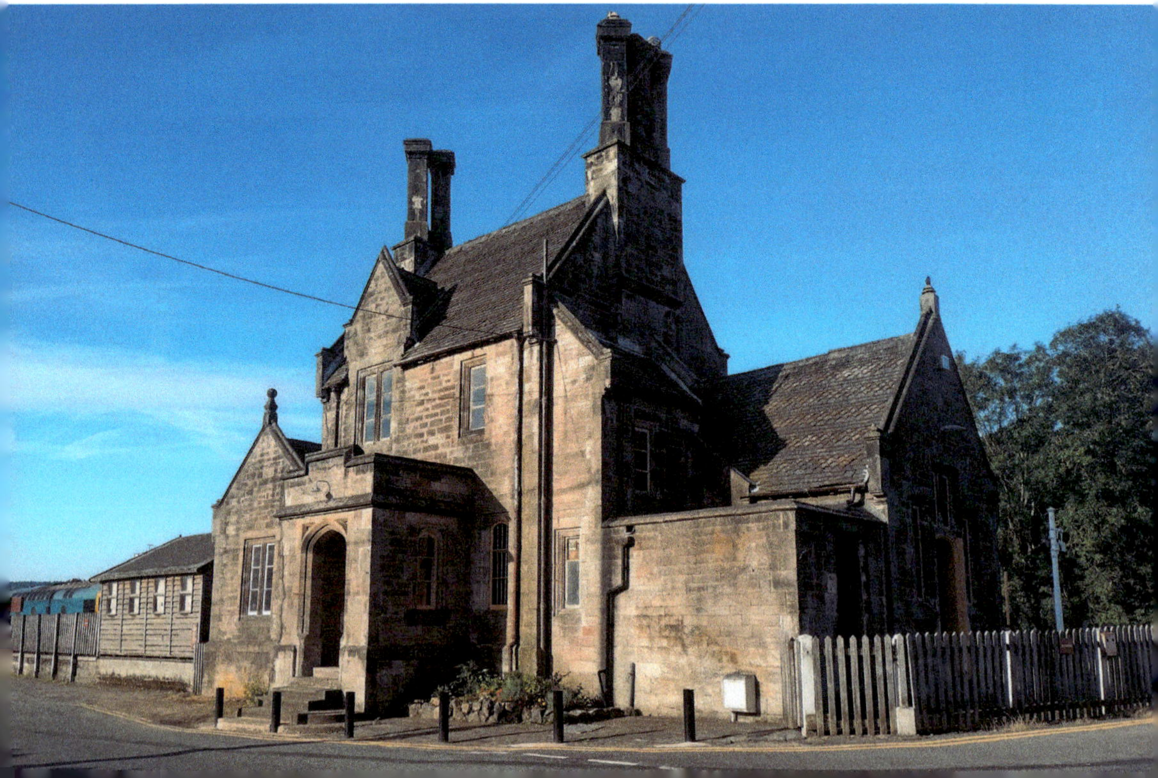

Bibliography and Further Reading

Baker, A. C., *The Cheadle Railway* (St Albans: Oakwood Press, 1979)

Christiansen, R., and R. W. Miller, *The North Staffordshire Railway* (Newton Abbot: David & Charles, 1971)

Dawson, A. L., *The Early Railways of Manchester* (Stroud: Amberley Publishing, 2017)

Dow, G., *North Staffordshire Album* (London: Ian Allan, 1970)

Guy, A., 'The Missing Link: Some Atypical Early Railways in Britain' in D. Gwyn (ed.) *Early Railways 5* (Six Martlets, 2014), pp. 171–198

Hopkins, K., *North Staffordshire Locomotives* (Burton on Trent: Trent Valley Publications: 1986)

'Manifold', *The North Staffordshire Railway* (Ashbourne: J. H. Henstock Ltd, 1952)

Patel, R., *The Lane End Plateway* (Catrine: Oakwood Press, 2019)

The Illustrated London News

The National Archives, Kew: North Staffordshire Railway. RAIL 532/3 to 532/9 Directors' Meetings, 1846–1923

The Railway Magazine

The Staffordshire Advertiser

The Staffordshire Sentinel

Acknowledgements

This book was written to mark the centenary of the end of the North Staffordshire Railway, known to many as the 'Owd Knotty', in July 1923. The story of the 'Knotty' is one of a tenacious fight for survival against threats external and internal, but also one of individualism and innovation. In writing this book I'd like to thank Andrew Mason for his continuing support of my writing endeavours as well as his excellent graphics and checking the text. I'd also like to thank Richard and Johnathan Garside for reading through drafts of the manuscript. Thanks also to members of the museum team at the Foxfield Railway, to Richard Warren (Knotty Coach Trust) and to Mark Smith (Chairman Knotty Coach Trust and of the North Staffordshire Railway Study Group) for their support, and to the latter for use of images in the study group collection.